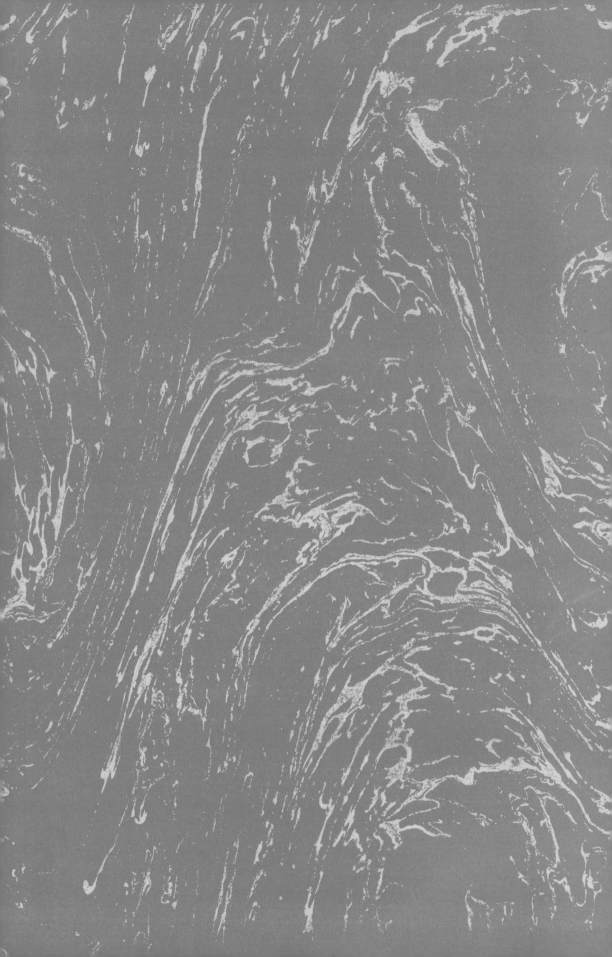

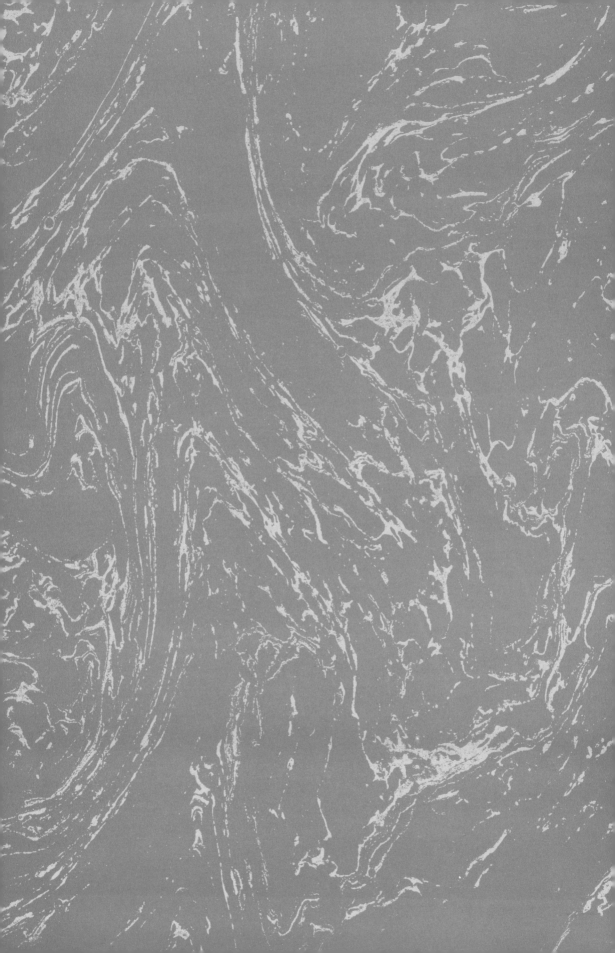

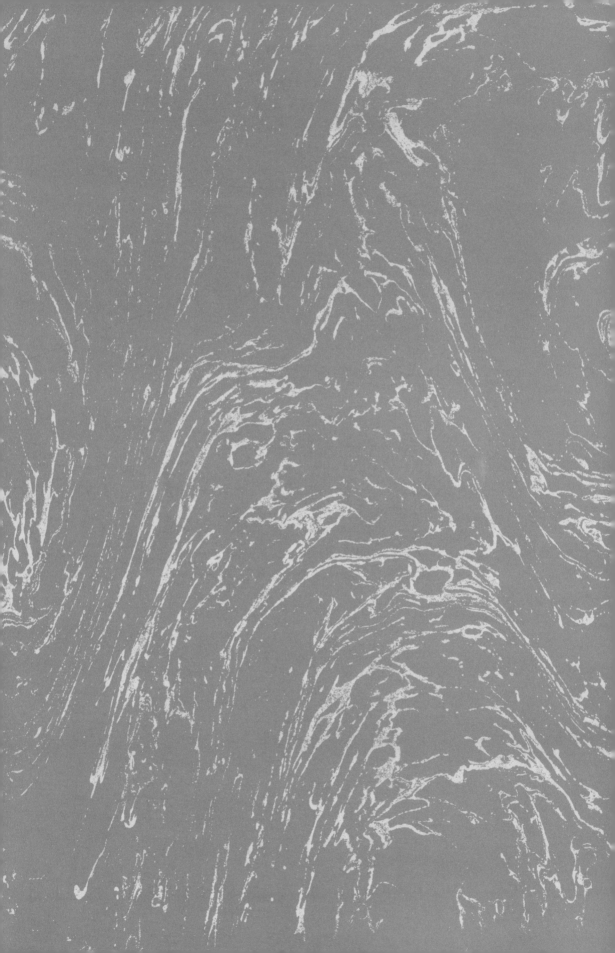

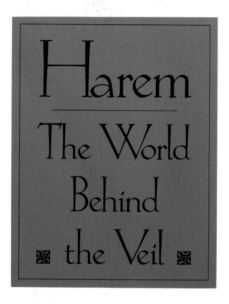

Harem

The World
Behind
the Veil

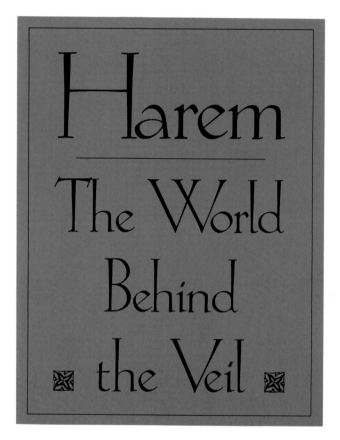

Harem
The World
Behind
the Veil

Alev Lytle Croutier

Abbeville Press · Publishers

New York · London · Paris

Editor: Alan Axelrod
Designer: Renée Khatami
Picture editor: Elizabeth Peyton
Production editor: Amy Handy
Production supervisor: Hope Koturo

Library of Congress Cataloging-in-Publication Data
Croutier, Alev Lytle, 1944–
  Harem: the world behind the veil/
Alev Lytle Croutier.
    p.   cm.
  Bibliography: p.
  Includes index.
  ISBN 1-55859-159-1
  1. Harem—History.   2. Women—Islamic countries—History.   3. Women—Turkey—History.   I. Title.
HQ1170.C84   1989
305.4'2'0917671—dc 19   88-32733

Jacket front: *Jean-Auguste Dominique Ingres, La Grande Odalisque. See p. 180.*

Jacket back: *Woman wearing a yashmak and carrying a chanta, Collection of the author*

Frontispiece: *Unknown artist, Harem Scene at Court of Shah Jahan (album leaf), second quarter of 17th century (detail), Ink, colors and gold on paper, 7⅞ x 5 in. (13⅛ x 8¼ in. sheet), The Metropolitan Museum of Art, New York; Theodore M. Davis Collection, Bequest of Theodore M. Davis, 1915*

Dedication page: *Harem Dancer. The woman watching her from behind the lattice window is wearing a burqu, the face veil once commonly seen on urban Egyptian women.*

Table of Contents: *Silk Embroidery, Istanbul(?), possibly late 16th–17th century, The Textile Museum, Washington, D.C. (1.22)*

pages 14–15: *Velvet Cushion Cover, Istanbul, 17th century, The Textile Museum, Washington, D.C. (1.54)*

pages 142–43: *Velvet, Bursa, possibly 2nd half of 15th or 16th century, The Textile Museum, Washington, D.C. (1.77)*

pages 170–71: *Velvet, Bursa or Istanbul, 2nd half of 16th–early 17th century, The Textile Museum, Washington, D.C. (1.53)*

To all who
danced
the seven veils,
my mother
grandmothers
and aunts

Contents

Zehra Barutçu, my grandmother, about 1901

Preface

These flower-women, women-flowers, he prefers them to any others, and spends his nights in the hothouses where he hides them as in a harem.
—*Guy de Maupassant,* Un Cas de Divorce *(1886)*

I was born in a *konak* (old house), which once was the harem of a pasha. During my childhood, servants and odalisques lived there with us. I grew up in Turkey, listening to stories and songs that could easily have come from the *One Thousand and One Nights*. People around me often whispered things about harems; my own grandmother and her sister had been brought up in one. Since then, I have come to see that these were not ordinary stories. But for me, as a child, they were, for I had not yet known any others.

My paternal grandmother, Zehra, was the first person from whom I heard the word *harem* and who made allusions to harem life. She was the daughter of a wealthy gunpowder maker in Macedonia. As was the custom until the twentieth century, she and her sisters had been brought up in a "harem," or a separate part of a house where women were isolated; the only men they encountered were their blood relatives. On rare occasions they went out, always heavily veiled. Sometimes silk tunnels were stretched from the door of the house to a carriage, so that the women could leave without being seen from the street. Their marriages had already been arranged by the family. None of them saw their husbands until their wedding day. Then they moved to his house, to live together with their mother-in-law and his other women relatives.

My grandmother married my grandfather when she was fourteen. He was forty and her father's best friend. She was a simple, uneducated girl. He was a respected scholar. Ten years later, she was widowed. With one of her sisters, she moved into her brother-in-law's harem; and there the two sisters brought their children up together, as one family.

Threatened by the Balkan Wars, they left everything behind in Macedonia, including their parents, and fled to Anatolia. They sought refuge and settled down in Istanbul in 1906. They were among the last women who had lived in harems; in 1909, with the fall of Abdulhamid, harems were abolished and declared unlawful.

I do not remember very much of the house in Izmir (Smyrna) where I was born. It faced the sea, was five stories high, and it had a *hamam* (bath house) where groups of women came to bathe. A giant granite rock behind the house isolated it from the world. It was said that before us, an old pasha, his two wives, and other women occupied the place. As a child, I played dress-up with embroidered clothes that the women from another era had left behind.

In 1950, with my parents and grandmother, I moved to an apartment house in Ankara that was inhabited by assorted family members. We lived

Meryem, my great-aunt, with her husband, Faik Pasha, and daughters (clockwise), Muazzez, Mukaddes, and Ayhan. Faik Pasha made a gift of orphan odalisques to my family.

Sadri and Yümniye Aksoy, my father and mother, in Turkish costume, 1942

as an extended family—two uncles, three aunts, my grandmother, my great-aunt, many cousins, and *odalisques* (servant girls) who were gifts from my great-uncle, Faik Pasha, and owned by the family. He had found them in a cave after their parents had been killed in a border dispute near Iran. The Ottoman palaces were gone, but not the need to live as one big family: clustered apartments were occupied by large families.

When the women gathered together, the old sisters told stories and argued about facts and details, occasionally agreeing on some. We all participated in rituals, vanishing rites the sisters had transported from their harem days. We learned to make concoctions to remove hair, brew good coffee, distribute a sacrificed sheep's entrails to the poor, cast spells, and give the evil eye to protect ourselves. These were the origins of my exposure to harem life, accepted as part of a prosaic existence.

When I was eighteen years old, I left Turkey and came to live in the United States. In 1978, fifteen years later, I returned to Istanbul to visit my family and sort out my impressions of my birthplace. I returned, carrying new baggage with me: an expatriate's eye and a self-conscious awareness of art history and of feminist rhetoric. It was not surprising, then, that I found myself fascinated with the recently opened harem apartments of Topkapi Palace—the Grand Seraglio, or the Sublime Porte, as it was known in the West. It had belonged to the *sultans* (emperors) of the Ottoman Dynasty, who had kept their women hidden away here from around 1540 through the early 1900s—four hundred years of life and culture. All that remained now of the thousands of women who had lived in these rooms, in fantastic luxury and isolation, were their empty boudoirs, their echoing baths, and countless, impenetrable mysteries.

Opposite left:
Nesime and Sevim,
my great cousins

Opposite right:
My aunts Muazzez
and Mukaddes
(dressed in a World
War I army uniform).
Since, during the
early twentieth
century, it was
usually inappropriate
for women to be
photographed with
men, some posed with
other women dressed
in men's clothes.

Opposite below:
Aunt Ayhan with
baby Genghiz.
Ayhan was the
beauty in the family.
Even Kemal Atatürk,
Turkey's great
reformer and first
president, admired
her.

This visit to the harem of the Topkapi Palace haunted me. I was obsessed with the notion that these same stairways once felt the flying feet, these alleys, the soft rustle of their garments. The walls seemed to whisper secrets pleading to be heard. The marble floors of the baths seemed to echo centuries of pouring water. Obviously, more was concealed here than the popular notion of sensuality attached to the word *harem* and what I had been exposed to as a child. It seemed as though I had stepped into a unique and extraordinary reality—a cocoon of women in their evolutionary cycle. Questions kept insinuating themselves. What had happened here during all these years? Who were these women? What did they do from day to day?

I began searching in earnest for documents on harems—books, letters, travelogues, paintings, photographs—to help reconstruct a candid image of this veiled world. What I found were fragments—romanticized descriptions of the imperial harem by Western travelers, writers, and diplomats, a few smuggled letters and poems written by the women themselves, and tedious studies by historians whose primary interest was royal life and palace politics, not the uncounted, unnamed women of the harem.

Simultaneously I had to probe deeper into my own family history. When I expressed my need to find out everything about harems, on which nothing definitive had been written, many of my relatives and friends came forth. They helped me remember things. They showed me strange books and letters. They shared ephemeral stories, things that had happened a long time ago, so that I could write about them.

Physical and spiritual isolation of women, and polygamy, I discovered, were not unique to Turkey. Harems existed throughout history in different parts of the Asian world, known by different names, such as *purdah* ("curtain") in India and, in Persia, *enderun* or *zenane*. In China, the Forbidden City of Peking also had cloistered women and used eunuchs to protect and guard them. But the most highly and extensively developed harem was that of the Grand Seraglio. What happened there came to be seen as the paradigm of all harems.

In the Seraglio alone, thousands of women lived and died with only each other to know of their lives. By piecing together the fragments collected over the years, I hoped to discover this mysterious, beautiful, and unbelievably repressive world concealed for so many centuries behind the veil. What will these women tell us, about themselves and about ourselves?

The Grand Harem

Intro-duction

I am a harem woman, an Ottoman slave. I was conceived in an act of contemptuous rape and born in a sumptuous palace. Hot sand is my father; the Bosphorus, my mother; wisdom, my destiny; ignorance, my doom. I am richly dressed and poorly regarded; I am a slave-owner and a slave. I am anonymous, I am infamous; one thousand and one tales have been written about me. My home is this place where gods are buried and devils breed, the land of holiness, the backyard of hell. —Anonymous

Meaning

The word *harem,* derived from the Arabic *haram* (حرم), means "unlawful," "protected," or "forbidden." The sacred area around Mecca and Medina is haram, closed to all but the Faithful. In its secular use, *harem* refers to the separate, protected part of a household where women, children, and servants live in maximum seclusion and privacy. *Harem* also applies to the women themselves and can allude to a wife. Finally, *harem* is "House of Happiness," a less-than-religious acceptance of the master's exclusive rights of sexual foraging, a place where women are separated and cloistered, sacrosanct from all but the one man who rules their lives. It is a place in a noble and rich house, guarded by eunuch slaves, where the lord of the manor keeps his wives and concubines.

Origins

Harem, a world of isolated women, is the combined result of several traditions. It suggests a clear idea of the separation between things, the sublime duality of the sacred and profane, whereby reality is divided into mutually exclusive categories and controlled by strict regulations known as taboos. Under such a system, men and women are among the first to be divided. Women symbolize passion; men, reason. Eve was the temptress, and patriarchal systems throughout the ages have tended to regard all women as such.

Scripture notwithstanding, there was a world before the time of Adam and Eve—in some places, a prepatriarchal world. In Sumerian, Egyptian, and Greek civilizations, for instance, women occupied high positions of spiritual power and ascended to the thrones of the gods. Under these sys-

Jean-Léon Gérôme, The Slave Market, n.d., Oil on canvas, 33³/₁₆ x 24¹³/₁₆ in., Sterling and Francine Clark Art Institute, Williamstown, Massachusetts

tems, which were essentially matriarchal, both female and male deities controlled the destinies of human beings and animals. They were equally powerful.

The white goddess of birth, love, and death is the earliest-known deity. She was personified as the moon, full, new, and old, and was worshiped under infinite names, as Isis, Ishtar, Artemis, and others. She was the Great Goddess in her multifarious forms.

At the dawn of civilization, clans migrated continually in search of food and game, everyone collaborating in a tribal act. In this set-up, the forms of subsistence left no surplus, and the concepts of private ownership, class distinction, masters and slaves did not exist.

As agriculture began to provide a more reliable source of food than hunting and gathering, endless migration became less essential for survival. Tribes rooted down, claiming land and territory. At first, incarnations of the connection between seeds and growing things, women rose to a privileged position in early societies. So did the female deities. Demeter, the Greek goddess of fertility, protected the crops; had she not been compelled to share her daughter, Persephone, with the male underworld, there would have been perpetual—rather than merely seasonal—abundance.

Eventually, agricultural knowledge created a surplus of food for some, making it possible to exploit others who did not have the means to secure their own subsistence. The ownership of private property, especially land, replaced communal sharing, splitting society into landowners and varying degrees of slaves. This development was concurrent with the decline of women's spiritual prestige; they ceased performing religious rituals. The mother was no longer the axis of the family; the father became the *paterfamilias*. In ancient Rome, *familia* meant a man's fields, property, money, and slaves, all of which were passed on to his sons. Woman became part of man's *familia,* his property. And polygamy was established as an important part of an economic system in which a man needed many hands to maintain his livelihood.

The story of Adam and Eve appears in Judaism as a demonstration that woman is sinful and that her sin is sex. The story affirms a severance of body from soul, which Christianity embraced and exaggerated by representing Christ as a holy male born of a woman who had conceived asexually; Christ was so chaste that he was deprived of women and sexual expression.

This cornerstone of Judeo-Christian belief divided human beings from themselves, opposing to a humanitarian conviction of the essential goodness of the body, inherited from ancient Egyptian and Greco-Roman religions, a

Odalisque, *early*
17th century,
Miniature from the
Murabba Album,
Topkapi Museum,
Istanbul. The woman
appears to be a
version of Eve,
with a pomegranate,
an ancient
fertility symbol.

belief that the physical reality of the here and now was to be despised in dreams of "another" world of infinite and insubstantial spirituality.

God had created man in his own image; God was spirit. But woman was the flesh or body, and the body was an animal dominated by passion, sensuality, and lust. Man personified the heavens, and woman could never be whole until married to one. By the thirteenth century, Thomas Aquinas and Albertus Magnus had promulgated their belief that women were capable of engaging in intercourse with Satan. On these grounds, the Inquisition identified and condemned certain women to be burned alive. Female spiritual submission was thus complete.

Men, on the other hand, allowed themselves plenty of sexual freedom under the patriarchal system. Prostitution increased rapidly; indeed, a large portion of the Catholic Church's income came from the brothels, and Martin Luther's Reformation was partly an attempt to end this hypocrisy. As for Islam, it imposed segregation and the veil upon women, claiming they could not be trusted and had to be kept away from men (other than close relatives), whom they could not help but seduce. The need for special, secluded dwelling places for women became imperative—not to protect their bodies and honor, but to preserve the morals of men.

Polygamy

Polygamy is the practice of having more than one spouse; in common usage, this means more than one wife. Founded on agrarian necessity, polygamy is part of many religions.

Islam holds women in particularly low esteem, considering them intellectually dull, spiritually vapid, valuable only to satisfy the passions of their masters and provide them male heirs. "Woman is a field, a sort of property that a husband may use or abuse as he sees fit," says the Koran, allowing four *kadins* (wives), if a man is able to keep them all in the same style and can share with them equal amounts of affection.

Mohammed had altruistic intentions when he sanctioned polygamy, seeing it as a solution to the pre-Islamic practice of female infanticide, as well as a practical way to deal with the surplus female population. It was mainly an economic measure, having little to do with Western romantic stereotypes.

In Arabic, the first wife is called *hatun* (the great lady) and the second, *durrah* (parrot). If a husband wants to get rid of any of his wives, he can divorce them with relative ease by saying, before a *kadi* (judge), "I divorce thee" three times. A wife cannot initiate a divorce; she has no rights. The

Koran also allows men to own as many *odalisques* (female slaves) as he pleases.

Multiple wives were expensive, not only to maintain, but also because it was the custom to raise a "bride price" for each wife. Poor men could barely afford one wife, although they sometimes took two anyway—separating the women in their poor home by a mere curtain. Wealthy men often exceeded the four "allowed" by the Koran and made a display of their wives as a status symbol. However, too much show attracted tax collectors and other undesirables.

Slave Markets

The slave market had been a thriving commerce in the Middle East and around the Mediterranean since Mesopotamian times, two thousand years before Christ. Young boys and girls, captured in war or paid as tribute by their fathers or local rulers, were available for purchase on the open market in all major cities. Alexandria and Cairo served as the main emporiums.

Many distinguished travelers and writers were fascinated by slave markets. Within a ten-year period, we hear varying descriptions:

> *The slave market was one of my favorite haunts. . . . One enters this building which is situated in a quarter the most dark, dirty and obscure of any at Cairo by a sort of lane. . . . In the center of this court, the slaves are exposed for sale and in general to the number of thirty to forty, nearly all young, many quite infants. The scene is of a revolting nature; yet I did not see as I expected the dejection and sorrow as I was led to imagine watching the master remove the entire covering of a female—a thick wollen cloth—and expose her to the gaze of the bystander.*
>
> William James Muller (1838), British Orientalist painter

> *Not the least of their attractions was their hair; arranged in enormous plaits, it was also entirely saturated in butter which streamed down their shoulders and breasts. . . . It was fashionable because it gave their hair more sheen, and made their faces more dazzling.*
>
> *The merchants were ready to have them strip: they poked open their mouths so that I could examine their teeth; they made them walk up and down and pointed out, above all, the elasticity of their breasts. These poor girls responded in the most carefree manner, and the scene was hardly a painful one, for most of them burst into uncontrollable laughter.*
>
> Gérard de Nerval, Voyage en Orient (1843–51)

When the dahabeeahs returned from their long and painful journeys on the Upper Nile, they install their human merchandise in those great okels which extend in Cairo along the ruined mosque of the Caliph Hakem; people go there to purchase a slave as they do here to the market to buy a turbot.

                  Maxime du Camp, Souvenirs et paysages d'Orient *(1849)*

Living in rooms opposite these slave girls, and seeing them at all hours of the day and night, I had frequent opportunities of studying them. They were average specimens of the steatopygous Abyssinian breed, broad-shouldered, thin-flanked, fine-limbed, and with haunches of a prodigious size. . . . Their style of flirtation was peculiar.

    "How beautiful thou art, O Maryam!—What eyes!—what—"

    "Then why—" would respond the lady—*"don't you buy me?"*

    "We are of one faith—of one creed, formed to form each other's happiness."

    "Then, why don't you buy me?"

    "Conceive, O Maryam, the blessing of two hearts."

    "Then, why don't you buy me?"

    and so on. Most effectual gag to Cupid's eloquence!

                  Sir Richard Burton, Personal Narrative of a Pilgrimage to Al-Madinah and Meccah *(1853)*

Edmund Dulac, Illustration to Quatrain XI of The Rubaiyat of Omar Kháyyám *(London: Hodder and Stoughton, 1909), Rare Book and Manuscript Library, Columbia University, New York.*

"With me along the Strip of Herbage strown That just divides the desert from the sown, Where name of Slave and Sultan is forgot— And peace to Mahmud on his golden throne?"

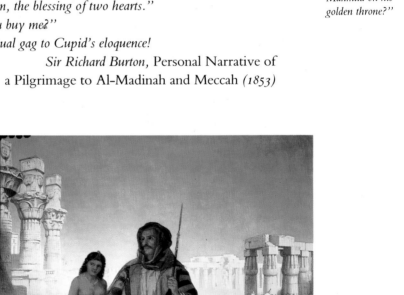

John Faed, Man Exchanging a Slave for Armor, *ca. 1858, Oil on board, 17¼ x 24 in., Private collection*

Harem of the Seraglio

The Turkish tribes, including the Ottomans, practiced polygamy prior to the conquest of the Byzantine capital, Constantinople, in 1453. Sultan Mehmed II, known to history as "the Conqueror," was obsessed with making his new metropolis, which he called Istanbul, a replica of Constantine's—only more opulent. He allowed the *valide sultana* (mother sultana) to organize her house as nearly as possible in the manner of the gynaecea (women's apartments) of Empress Helen, widow of Constantine. The gynaecea were situated in the remotest part of her palace, lying beyond an interior court; women lived here separately, divided into task groups. Mehmed himself adopted such Byzantine customs as the sequestering of royalty, establishing a palace school, and the keeping of household slaves. The Islamic practice of polygamy combined neatly with these Byzantine customs and resulted in the harem.

Gentile Bellini, Sultan Mehmet II, 1480, Oil on canvas, perhaps transferred from panel, 27½ x 20½ in., The National Gallery, London

A bird's-eye view of the Grand Harem of Topkapi Palace—the Seraglio. Photograph by Sami Güner

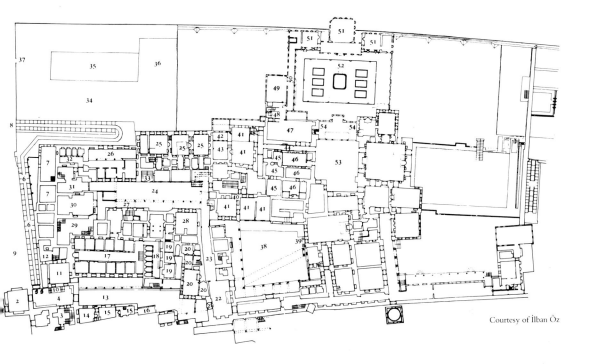

Courtesy of İlban Öz

Floor plan of the Grand Harem, Topkapi Palace

Key to plan

1. Carriage Gate
2. The Tower of Justice
3. Guard post before the Tower Door
4. Meskhane
5. Quarters of the halberdiers
6. Mounting block for the sultan
7. Mosque for the black eunuchs
8. Baths of the black eunuchs
9. Courtyard of the black eunuchs
10. Apartments of the black eunuchs
11. Quarters of the black eunuchs
12. Toilets of the black eunuchs
13. Princes' School
14. Main Gate
15. Second guard post of the Black Eunuchs
16. The Food Corridor
17. Courtyard of the kadins
18. Apartments of the kadins
19. Kitchen
20. Storeroom
21. Laundry
22. Harem Infirmary
23. Open Courtyard of the Infirmary
24. Quarters of the midwives, etc.
25. Death Gate
26. Courtyard of the valide sultana
27. Corridor of the valide sultana
28. Ground-floor apartments of the valide sultana
29. Bedroom of the valide sultana
30. Prayer Room of the valide sultana
31. Bath Corridor
32. Valide sultana's baths
33. The sultan's baths
34. Bedroom of Abdülhamid I
35. Stairs leading to the room of Selim III
36. Room of Selim III
37. Corridor leading to the Kiosk of Osman III
38. The Kiosk of Osman III
39. Hall of the Sultan
40. Corridor of the kadins
41. Apartments of the first kadin
42. Apartments of the second kadin
43. Hall of Murat III
44. The Kiosk of Murat III
45. The "Library" of Ahmet I
46. The Fruit Room of Ahmet III
47. Courtyard of the favorites
48. Apartments for the Haseki
49. Mabeyn
50. Boxwood Gardens
51. Open Pool
52. Golden Way
53. Mosque for the harem ladies
54. Kushane Gate

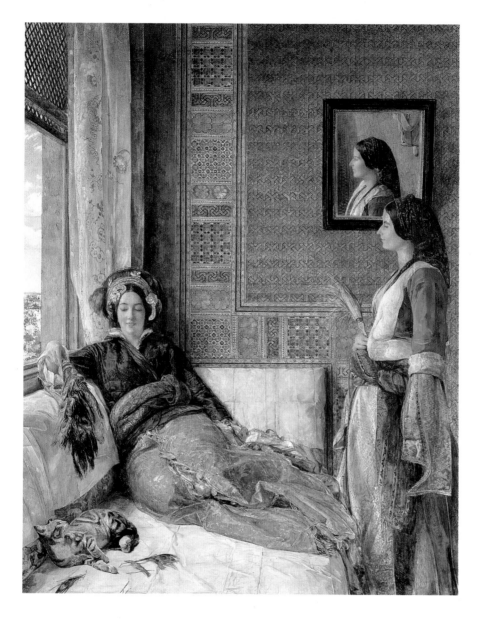

John Frederick Lewis
Hhareem Life,
Constantinople,
*1857, Oil on canvas,
Laing Art Gallery,
Newcastle, England*

The early Ottoman sultans had married daughters of Anatolian governors and of the Byzantine royal family. After the conquest of Constantinople, it became customary to marry odalisques. The women in harems, except those born in it, came from all over Asia, Africa, and, occasionally, Europe.

According to ancient legend, the Seraglio Point, a magnificent isthmus

John Frederick Lewis,
The Reception,
1873, Oil on panel,
25 x 30 in.,
Yale Center for
British Art, New
Haven, Connecticut;
Paul Mellon
Collection

extending between the Marmara Sea and the Golden Horn, was named by the Delphic Oracle as the best site for a new colony and became the Acropolis of ancient Byzantium. A decade after the conquest, Mehmed the Conqueror built Topkapi Palace—known in the West as the Grand Seraglio or the Sublime Porte—on the same sacred point.

In his poem "The Palace of Fortune" (1772), Sir William (Oriental) Jones invokes a palace of such opulence:

> *In mazy curls the flowing jasper wav'd*
> *O'er its smooth bed with polish'd agate pav'd;*
> *And on a rock of ice, by magick rais'd,*
> *High in the midst a gorgeous palace blaz'd.*

View of the Topkapi Palace and the Seraglio Point

The seraglio was the seat of imperial power, housing thousands of people involved in the sultan's personal and administrative service. The most private section, carefully separated from the rest of the palace, was the sultan's harem, which moved to the Seraglio for the first time in 1541, with Sultana Roxalena, and lasted until 1909. The ever-changing female family lived, loved, and died here for four centuries. It became the ultimate symbol, the quintessence of harem, the system of sequestering women.

The harem was located between the *Mabeyn* (Court)—the sultan's private apartments—and the apartments of the chief black eunuch. It had almost four hundred rooms centered around the Courtyard of the Valide Sultana, containing the apartments and dormitories of other women.

The Carriage House and the Bird House, which connected the harem to the outside world, were carefully guarded from within by the corps of eunuchs and, outside, by halberdiers, or royal guards. The Carriage House was the real entry to the harem; all contact with the outside was made through its gate, which opened at dawn and closed at dusk.

The eunuchs' quarters led into a courtyard, which opened on the right to the Golden Road, in the center to the valide sultana's quarters, and on the left to the apartments of the odalisques. The luxury of the living quarters depended on the status of the person occupying them. The sultan, of course, had the most magnificent accommodations. High-ranking women had private apartments. Novice odalisques and eunuchs lived in dormitories.

During the fifteenth and sixteenth centuries, the population of the harem dropped from over a thousand women to a few hundred, because the young princes were given governorships in various provinces and left the Seraglio, escorted by their own harems. After the seventeenth century, however, with reforms in the inheritance laws that allowed the princes to live in the palace with their own women—albeit as captives in the *Kafes* (the Golden Cage)—the harem population increased to almost two thousand.

At its zenith, the Ottoman Empire was enormous, stretching from the Caucasus Mountains to the Persian Gulf, from the Danube to the Nile. The history of the Seraglio and its harem symbolizes the fluctuating fortunes of the empire. The great expense of upkeep, the ruthless rivalry among the women, intrigues that influenced political affairs, and, ultimately, the exquisite beauty of these women of many nationalities fascinated the entire world. Everyone was curious to know what happened behind the harem walls— but no one was allowed behind them. Foreign ambassadors and artists reported accounts obtained from peddlers or servant women who had entered, but such narratives were often muddled by wishful exoticism. To this day, the reality is difficult to ascertain.

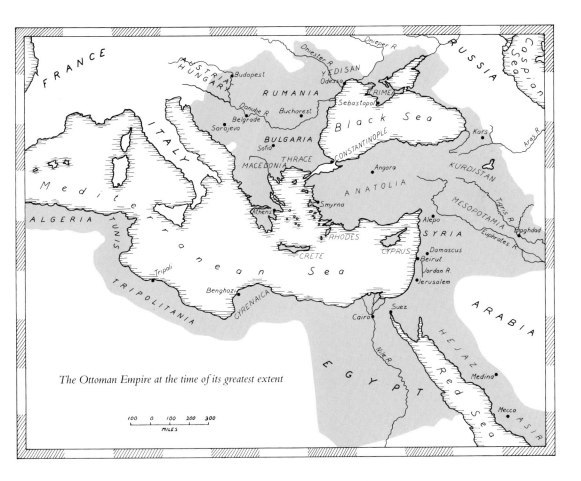

The Ottoman Empire at the time of its greatest extent

Acquisition of Slaves

Young girls of extraordinary beauty, plucked from the slave market, were sent to the sultan's court, often as gifts from his governors. Among the singular, lasting privileges of the valide sultana was the right to present her son with a slave girl on the Eve of Kurban Bayram (sacrificial day) each year.

The girls were all non-Moslems, uprooted at a tender age. The sultans were partial to the fair, doe-eyed beauties from the Caucasus region. Circassians, Georgians, and Abkhasians were proud mountain girls, believed to be the descendents of the Amazon women who had lived in Scythia near the Black Sea in ancient times and who had swept down through Greece as far as Athens, waging a war that nearly ended the city's glamorous history. Now *they* were being kidnapped or sold by impoverished parents. A customs declaration from around 1790 establishes their worth: "Circassian girl, about eight years old; Abyssinian virgin, about ten; five-year-old Circassian virgin, Circassian woman, fifteen or sixteen years old; about twelve-year-old Georgian maiden, medium tall negro slave, seventeen-year-old Negro slave. Costs about 1000–2000 kurush." In those days one could buy a horse for around 5000 kurush.

The promise of a life of luxury and ease overcame parental scruples against delivering their children into concubinage. Many Circassian and Georgian families encouraged their daughters to enter that life willingly: "Circassians take their own children to the market, as a way of providing for them handsomely . . . but the blacks and Abyssinians fight hard for their liberty," reported Lucie Duff Gordon in her 1864 travel diary.

Training of Odalisques

Before admitting these slave girls into the Seraglio harem, trained eunuchs carefully examined them for any physical defects or imperfections. If a girl were proclaimed satisfactory, the chief eunuch presented her to the valide sultana for approval. Once she was confined within the Seraglio, her Christian name would be changed to a Persian one that suited her particular qualities. If, for example, a young girl had beautiful rosy cheeks, she might be called Gulbahar, Rose of Spring. Now an odalisque, she was immediately converted to Islam and began an arduous training in palace etiquette and Islamic culture.

The word *odalisque* comes from *oda* (room) and means literally "woman

*Jean-Auguste
Dominique Ingres,*
Odalisque and
Slave, *1842,
Oil on canvas,
30 x 41½ in.
Walters Art Gallery,
Baltimore*

*Rudolph Ernst,
Idle Hours in the
Harem, c. 1900,
Oil on panel,
25⅜ x 32⅛ in.,
Private collection*

of the room," implying a general servant status. Odalisques with extraordinary beauty and talent were trained to become concubines, learning to dance, recite poetry, play musical instruments, and master the erotic arts. Twelve of the most attractive and gifted odalisques were selected as *gedikli* (maids-in-waiting) to the sultan, responsible for dressing and bathing him, doing his laundry, and serving his food and coffee. Gio Maria Angiolello, an Italian youth captured by Mehmed II and who stayed in the sultan's service until the sultan's death, wrote in his *Historia Turchesca* (1480) that these girls were taught writing and religion; they were also trained in a great many skills, including sewing, embroidery, playing the harp, and singing.

A tableau vivant representing harem life of the nineteenth century at the Topkapi Palace

If he were pleased, the sultan kept them for himself or ultimately gave them as gifts. Among the greatest honors he could bestow upon one of his pashas was to present him with an odalisque who had adorned his palace but had not yet become his concubine. According to Moslem etiquette, the pasha had to free the girl and make her his wife. Their courtly charms, as well as their important connections within the Seraglio, made these women very highly desirable.

Other odalisques were placed in the service of the valide sultana, the *kadins* (wives), the sultan's daughters, or the chief black and white eunuchs. Girls blessed with strong physiques became servants or administrators. Each novice was assigned to the *oda* of an important woman in charge of a particular harem department. These "cabinet ministers" included mistress of the robes, keeper of baths, keeper of jewels, reader of the Koran, keeper of the storerooms, mistress of sherbets, head of table service, and so on. It was possible for an odalisque to climb up the ladder of the harem hierarchy and achieve the highest ranks in the Imperial Harem. If, however, she lacked talent or manifested undesirable qualities, she was likely to be resold in the slave market.

Sultanas

The sultan was an almost godlike entity, before whom no one could speak or raise their eyes. Despite the legend that the sultan threw a handkerchief at the girl he intended to spend the night with, the choice of an odalisque, for the most part, was both less casual and less flamboyant. Often, a girl secretly accompanied the chief black eunuch into his majesty's chamber. Only after she earned high rank—becoming, for example, an *ikbal* (favorite)—would her relationship to the sultan be publicized, and only then would she be endowed with a private apartment, barge, carriage, and slaves. Seventeenth-century traveler Sir Paul Rycaut confirms this: "If the Sultan was pleased with the odalisque, he would put her, the next morning, under the custody of the Mistress of the House. She would be returned to the harem with just as pompous a ceremony as her admittance to the Sultan's bed. She would be bathed and moved into quarters worthy of a Haseki Sultana."

When a favorite gave birth to the sultan's child, she was elevated to the position of kadin or *haseki sultana*. If, perchance, the child was a boy and became the sultan, his mother became the ruler of the harem and the most powerful woman in the empire, the valide sultana. A Moslem man believed that heaven lay beneath his mother's feet. After all, he could have as many

Leon Bakst,
Odalisque.
*Costume design for
the Diaghilev ballet*
Schéhérazade,
*which featured the
legendary Karsavina
and Nijinsky, 1910.
Watercolor and gold
on paper, Private
collection*

wives and slaves as he wanted, but he had only one mother. He entrusted her with his most private and personal possessions—his women.

Competition for the coveted position of valide was vicious, and the stakes were high. Constant rivalries and feuds kept hearts pounding, brains alert. A seventeenth-century document in the Topkapi Palace archives speaks of the rivalry between Gülnush Sultana and the odalisque Gülbeyaz (Rosewhite), which led to a tragic end. Sultan Mehmed IV had been deeply enamoured of Gülnush, the haseki sultana, but after Gülbeyaz entered his harem, his affections began to shift. Gülnush, still in love with the sultan,

Leon Bakst, The Red Sultana, *1910, Watercolor, gouache, and gold on paper, Private collection*

became madly jealous. One day, as Gülbeyaz was sitting on a rock and watching the sea, Gülnush quietly pushed her off the cliff and drowned the young odalisque.

Royal motherhood provided immense power and wealth but very little security. To conceive was only to begin a perilous journey of self-defense, requiring great wit and courage. The prying eyes of jealous rivals were keen, and the threat to a mother's life and to the life of potential heirs was an everyday reality. A young prince stayed in the harem with his mother and nurses until he was twelve; during all this time his mother lived in constant anxiety. Kösem Sultana's conspiracy to assassinate the child sultan Mehmed IV and Roxalena's banishment of prince Mustafa, both of which will be discussed at length, are two examples.

With the ascension of a new sultan, the wives of his predecessor, along with their entourages, were sent to the Old Palace, known as the Palace of the Unwanted Ones or the House of Tears. Their apartments in the Seraglio were torn down, and new ones erected and decorated for the new occupants. Not that the new occupants were always satisfied with their accommodations, no matter how luxurious:

> Dearest Kalfa,
> I have heard from someone that she will be moving to the apartment which should be mine. No! As the earth is old, so do I want that apartment myself. I cannot bear a younger woman occupying such a spacious place, and if our mighty master heard my plea he wouldn't object. Please, convey this to the valide sultana with my deepest respects. Why should she move there and I stay where I am? I must insist on my seniority privileges. If this cannot be changed, I will simply not move to the Seraglio, I swear. But if she refuses to, that's a whole other affair. I will die rather than to let her have that beautiful apartment.
>
> Letter from Behice Sultana to the
> kalfa (mistress of the house) (1839)

Eunuchs

To guard their women, sultans retained an immensely valuable corps of eunuchs, at times as many as eight hundred strong. Eunuchs were male prisoners of war or slaves, castrated before puberty and condemned to a life of servitude. The white eunuchs served in the *Selâmlik*, where the sultan met with other men. The Golden Road, a lovely corridor with the most exquisite tilework, connected the Selâmlik to the harem, where the black eunuchs looked after the women. The chief black eunuch exercised great political power in court, serving as the most important link between the sultan and his mother. Officially his position was as important as that of the grand vezier (prime minister).

Because they were often privy to the most intimate secrets of the harem and also had access to the outer world, the eunuchs became the most corrupt element in palace society. Surrounded by women trained to arouse passion in men, they spent their lives forever confronted by the loss of sexual capability. Many became skillful intriguers, translating their resentment into vengeance. We find such a creature in Montesquieu's *Persian Letters:*

> *The Seraglio is my Empire; and my ambition, the only passion left me, finds no small gratification. I mark with pleasure that my presence is required at all times; I willingly incur the hatred of all these women, because it establishes me more firmly in my post. And they do not hate me for nothing, I can tell you: I interfere with their most innocent pleasures; I am always in the way, an insurmountable obstacle; before they know where they are, they find their schemes frustrated.*

The palace dwarf, also a eunuch, was kind of a court jester, a great source of amusement for the sultan and ladies of the harem. Because he presented little threat, he often was included in the most private and intimate situations. For example, Levni's *Zanan-Name,* an eighteenth-century notebook of miniatures depicting life in the Seraglio, contains a dwarf among the female attendants, entertaining a woman as she gives birth.

Dynasty

The laws of inheritance decreed that the sultanate pass to the oldest living male member of the family, rather than from father to son. Mehmed the Conqueror, well-versed in court intrigue, formulated the regulations that governed Ottoman policies for centuries. He sanctioned a sultan's killing his male relatives to secure his throne for his own offspring—which resulted in such atrocities as the murder of Mehmed III's nineteen brothers in 1595, some of them infants, at the instigation of his mother, or the stuffing into sacks of seven of Mehmed's father's pregnant concubines and throwing them into the Sea of Marmara. "After the burial of the princes, the populace gathered in crowds outside the palace to watch their mothers and the other wives of the dead sultan leave the palace. All the coaches, carriages, horses, mules of the palace were employed for this purpose. Besides the wives of the sultan, his twenty-seven daughters and over two hundred odalisques under the protection of eunuchs were taken to the Old Palace. . . . There, they could cry as much as they wished in mourning for their dead sons," reports Ambassador H. G. Rosedale, in *Queen Elizabeth and the Levant Company* (1604).

The Golden Cage

In 1666, Selim II issued an edict softening the Conqueror's cruel decree. Selim II's order allowed the imperial princes to survive, but not to participate in public activities during the life of the reigning sovereign. From then on, the princes were kept secluded in the *Kafes* (Golden Cage), an apartment adjoining the harem but separated from it by a gate called the *Djinn's Kapi* (Genie's Gate), which was off-limits to everyone else in the harem.

The princes spent their lives in isolation, except for a few concubines who had been sterilized by removal of ovaries or uterus. If, through some oversight, any woman did become pregnant by an outcast prince, she was immediately drowned. Guards, whose eardrums had been perforated and tongues slit, served the princes. These deaf-mutes were guardians—as well as potential assassins.

Life in the Golden Cage was racked by fear and suffused in ignorance of events outside. At any time, the sultan or palace rebels might kill everyone. If a prince lived long enough to ascend to the throne, he was, more often than not, unprepared to rule an empire. When Murad IV died in 1640, his successor Ibrahim I was so terrified of the crowd trying to enter the Cage to proclaim him sultan that he barred the door and would not come out until Murad's dead body was placed before him. Suleyman II, during the thirty-nine years he spent in the Kafes, became an ascetic and a master calligrapher. Later, as sultan, he frequently manifested a desire to return to his former isolation and solitude. Other princes, like Ibrahim I, indulged in spasms of violent debauchery, seeking vengeance for their lost years. In the Cage, the slave system on which the Seraglio depended consumed its masters, turning *them* into slaves.

Death

Many of the women in the harem died young. There are endless stories of brutal murders and poisonings. Henry Lello, English ambassador to the Ottoman court in 1600, declared it was impossible to enumerate the intrigues of the harem. Many women were drowned. Those to be murdered were seized by the chief black eunuch, who stuffed them in sacks, tied the neck tightly, and loaded them in a rowboat. After rowing out from the shore a little way, the eunuch assisted in throwing the sacks overboard.

In 1665, some harem women in the court of Mehmed IV, accused of stealing the jewels from the cradle of one of the royal infants, started a fire to cover up the theft. The fire caused considerable damage in the harem and other parts of the Seraglio. These women were immediately strangled by order of the sultan.

Mehmed the Conqueror killed his own wife Irene with a stroke of his scimitar. Irene became a martyr, and, like all martyrs, she was proclaimed a saint and consigned to paradise. "The fortunate fair who has given pleasure to her lord will have the privilege of appearing before him in paradise," says the Koran. "Like the crescent moon, she will preserve all her youth and her husband will never look older or younger than thirty-one years." Mehmed may have been remembering these words when he took Irene's life.

The World of Extremes

The Grand Seraglio, the Golden Cage, and the harem were worlds of extremes—frightened women plotting with men who were not men against absolute rulers who kept their relatives immured for decades. The setting was rife with conflict, and frequent tragedies touched the innocent as well as the guilty. The sultan, or *padishah,* known as the King of Kings, the Unique Arbiter of the World's Destinies, the Master of the Two Continents and the Two Seas, and Sovereign of the East and the West, was himself the product of a union between a king and a slave woman. His sons and the entire Ottoman dynasty shared the same fate—kings born of slave mothers, procreating offspring with more slave mothers.

The Orientals viewed these rapid changes in fortune, the flirtation of good and evil, as the workings of *kismet* (fate). They believed that everyone's personal destiny had already been shaped by a divine being. Whether tragedy or luck touched life, it was kismet. The universal acceptance of kismet among slaves as well as royalty explains the acquiesce to the deprivations, tortures, and sudden misfortunes that occurred daily in the harem.

The common suffering often led to tremendous compassion among the inmates of the exalted household. In the harem, deep bonds developed alongside jealousies and rivalries among women who loved and cared for one another. To survive the turmoil and intrigue, they built strong and trusting relationships. These bonds are the harem's most touching secrets.

All that remains now of these women's lives are latticed windows, labyrinthine corridors, marbled baths, and dusty divans. Still, tales of the women behind the veil live on, an echo of the pathos and the pleasure of the *One Thousand and One Nights,* a part of our memory and also a part of tonight.

Daily Life in the Sultan's Harem

And slender-waisted [maidens] would visit us after the rest from their chambers, Plump their buttocks, wearing rings upon their waists, Shining their faces, closely veiled, restraining their glances, dark-eyed, Luxuriating in [heavenly] bliss, drenched in ambergris, Sweeping along the robes of [their] charms, and undergarments, and silk, Never seeing the sun save as a pendant [glimpsed] through the gaps of [their] curtains. . . . —Abu'l-Atahiya (748–825), Arab poet; translation by A. J. Arberry

Harem Walls

The old Turkish proverb, "Our private lives must be walled" was a metaphor for all of Ottoman society. Harems walled women literally. The historian Dursun Bey wrote, "If the sun had not been female [*shems,* the word for sun, is feminine], even she would never have been allowed to enter the harem." Actually, Gülbeyaz, favorite of Mehmed IV, wrote in the seventeenth century that "The sun never visits us. My skin is like ivory."

Intimacies rarely found their way outside the walls; we have very few firsthand accounts of day-to-day life in the harem. To gain a sense of its domestic pace and more private rhythms, it becomes necessary to assemble fragments from numerous, often contradictory, sources. But a beguiling image does slowly materialize.

In the painting *The White Slave* by Lecomte de Nouy, a dark-haired beauty smokes a cigarette while she stares into empty space. What does she do on any given day, one day in an endless series melting into months and years, with only the harem walls to witness the passage of her life? What about the chocolate-colored girl in the background, squeezing out a towel? What is she thinking about? In *A New Light in the Harem,* by Frederick Goodall, a woman reclines on a divan while a black nurse amuses a naked baby with a birdlike toy. What are this reclining woman's dreams? Is she the child's mother, whose life depends on the whim of one all-powerful ruler, the sultan, and one all-powerful God, Allah?

How many of the harem women accepted kismet—"written in their foreheads," according to the Koran—after being captured or bought as slaves and forced to convert to Islam? We know from a collection of letters written by various sultanas, *Harem'den Mektuplar* (1450–1850), that there

Jean-Jules-Antoine Lecomte de Nouy, The White Slave, 1888, Oil on canvas, 57½ x 46½ in., Musée des Beaux-Arts, Nantes, France

were literate women in the harem who never mastered the language of their captors. Did Christian and Jewish women secretly pray to their God, begging for deliverance from the punishment He had visited upon them? Did they live with the shame of believing their souls could never be redeemed? We will never know for sure.

We have evidence that the black arts were practiced in the harem. Fortune-telling, magic, and Cabalism all had their secret and overt adepts, looking for ways to predict the future, to ease the present, and to exorcise the demons incubating within.

And we hear of the rebels, women who succumbed to the passions of their hearts, risking affairs and plotting clandestine rendezvous with their lovers. In the harem of the Seraglio, there is a beautiful lacquered closet and a moving tale that goes along with it.

Sultan Ahmed II learns that one of his odalisques has been carrying on with a handsome youth who has been entering the harem surreptitiously. The sultan, enraged, lays a trap for the lovers. Taken by surprise, they flee in terror through the corridors of the harem with the sultan in hot pursuit. When they reach the quarters of the black eunuchs, the pair disappears into a closet. The sultan follows them, dagger drawn. He opens the closet, intending to dispose of both the unfaithful odalisque and the daring intruder.

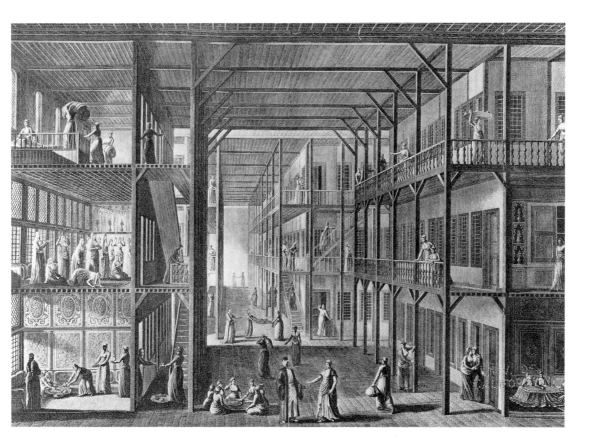

The Harem in Topkapi Palace, from "Codex Vindobonensis," late 16th century, Watercolor, Austrian National Library, Vienna

To his astonishment, the closet is empty. No sign of the lovers anywhere. Convinced that a miracle has occurred, the sultan falls to his knees and breaks into tears. He has the sacred closet decorated with gold and made into a shrine.

But divine intercession rarely came for violators of harem rules. Countless unfortunates lie at the bottom of the Bosphorus and the Sea of Marmara, betrayed by spies, the lies of rivals, or mere slips of the tongue made in idle gossip.

Everything that happened behind the harem walls was tempered by a certain knowledge that once a woman passed through the Gates of Felicity into the harem, there was no returning. The outside world ceased to exist. Let us step now through those gates, into the House of Felicity, the sultan's harem in Topkapi Palace.

Alphonse-Etienne Dinet, Moonlight at Laghouat ("Clair de lune à Laghouat"), 1897, Oil on canvas, 18¼ x 28⅝ in., Musée Saint-Denis, Reims, France

Gardens

The gardens were exquisite, surrounded by a forest of plane trees and cypresses, filled with roses, jasmine, and verbena. Footpaths led to tiny ponds

John Frederick
Lewis, In the Bey's
Garden, Asia
Minor, *1865*,
Oil on canvas,
42 x 27 in.,
Harris Museum
and Art Gallery,
Preston, England

with floating waterlilies and exotic fish, to gilded gazebos and kiosks meant to shade the stroller from the sun. The gardens were a special playground for the women, some taking pleasure in gardening, others simply cherishing a lazy promenade on a warm day. Followed by an entourage of odalisques and eunuchs, the favorites wandered the paths, picking flowers and fruit, eating kebabs and halvah, playing childlike games. In his 1766 account, *Observations sur le commerce,* Jean-Claude Flachat describes such an outing: "When everything is ready, the sultan calls for *halvet* [the seclusion of the area]. All the gates opening onto the palace gardens are closed. The Bostanjis [Sultan's bodyguards] keep sentinel duty outside, and the eunuchs inside. Sultanas come out of the harem and follow the sultan into the garden. Women pour from all directions, like swarms of bees flying from the hive in search of honey, and pausing when they find a flower."

Games

Most of the games the odalisques played seem extremely unsophisticated and simpleminded, intended more for small children than grown women—but then, the average age in the harem was seventeen. In a game called

A. Passini,
Promenade of the
Harem, *n.d.,*
Lithograph,
6½ x 10½ in.,
Collection of the
author

"Istanbul Gentlemen," for example, one of the women dressed as a man, her eyebrows thickened with *kohl,* a moustache painted on, a carved watermelon or pumpkin placed on her head as a hat, and a fur coat reversed and slipped on. She sat on a donkey, facing backwards, one hand holding the tail and the other prayer beads made of onion or garlic cloves. Someone kicked the donkey, and off she went, giggling and trying to maintain her balance in a kind of primitive rodeo.

Another popular game was a form of tag. One of the girls fell into a pool, pretending she had slipped. As she struggled to climb out, the others tried pushing her back in. If, at last, she managed to get out, she chased after the other women, trying to push them into the water. The sultan watched this childish spectacle from his private quarters, often selecting his next favorite.

In another game, which outlasted the harem itself, one of the girls was blindfolded and the others asked, "Beauty or ugliness?" The blindfolded girl chose one or the other while the girls struck poses of ugliness or beauty.

Anton Ignaz Melling,
Second View of the
Bosphorous, taken
from Kandilly,
Etching reproduced
in Views of
Constantinople and
the Bosphorous,
ca. 1815

When the time was up, she removed the blindfold and selected her favorite, who started the ritual all over again.

The sultan's young daughters played with Circassian slave girls they had received as gifts, like live dolls, bathing them, braiding their hair, making clothes for them with the help of their own royal mothers. They taught them things that only a princess should know. When these child-dolls grew up, they often became the attendants of the princesses, accompanying them into their new homes after the princesses were married.

Pools

During the hot and humid summer months, the women amused themselves in a large marble pool, containing small *kayiks* (row boats). In another pool they splashed and lounged while black eunuchs kept guard. Murad III, reknowned as a womanizer exceptional even among sultans, watched from behind the arabesques as the naked girls frolicked in the water. Often he would invent new games for them. These hours of passionate voyeurism

Jean-Léon Gérôme, Terrace of the Seraglio, 1886?, Photogravure, 7 x 10 in., Collection of the author

Conrad Kiesel,
The Daughters
of the Sheik,
ca. 1889,
Photogravure,
8 x 11½ in.,
Collection of the
author

must have had a stimulating effect, for Murad III sired one hundred and three children.

Ibrahim I would throw pearls and rubies into the water, enticing the girls to dive for them. During his reign, the chief black eunuch bought himself a beautiful slave girl. She was sold to him as a virgin, but shortly after she entered the harem her belly started to grow, and she soon gave birth to a little boy. About the same time, Turhan Sultana, the first kadin, also gave birth to a boy. The slave girl was employed as the wet nurse for the young prince Mehmed and moved into the royal harem with her baby son. The sultan was so taken with this healthy and robust little boy, who seemed like such a contrast to his own anemic and fragile son, that he began neglecting the little prince and spending his time playing with and favoring the slave girl's son. Turhan Sultana was most upset with this shift of affection and complained. Ibrahim was enraged. He tore the young prince from his mother's arms and threw him into the pool. Mehmed survived, but he was to carry a scar on his forehead until the end of his life.

Riddles and Stories

It is easy to picture the women taking their leisure by the pools, endlessly chatting with each other for diversion, playing childish games, talking of *cennet* (heaven) and *cehennem* (hell), telling tales of fairies and giants. Younger women were spellbound by the narratives of old crones, who would recite legends from Persian literature and love stories such as *Leyla and Mejnun,* a transcendental tale of the search for the loved and lost, who often appeared in animal forms.

The storytelling ritual always ended with, "Three apples have fallen from the sky; one belongs to the storyteller, the second to the listeners, and the third to me." The "me" is presumably the protagonist of the story, with whom everyone identified.

After sunset and before sunrise, women were not allowed outdoors. That's when the stories were born. One legend holds that in order to ease their insomnia, the women told stories to each other. They also enjoyed asking riddles, which all seemed to end with a threat to life and a flirtation with death. A perpetual danger loomed over the harem:

> *Yellow like saffron,*
> *Reads like the Koran;*
> *Either you'll solve this riddle,*
> *Or tonight your death will take you.*

This riddle is supposed to have originated in the fifteenth century. It was asked by an older woman of a prepubescent girl, as part of a rite of passage. When my great aunt asked it of me—I was ten years old—I could not for the life of me think of an answer. All evening, I was mortified that Azrael, the angel of death, was peeking over my left shoulder. My grandmother, sensing my terror, whispered "gold" in my ear, thereby delivering me from premature expiration.

Poetry

The most common craft practiced by the women was poetry. Their dissociation from the world, the surroundings, the quality and pace of their secluded existence lent themselves to poetic expression. Tragedy, suffering, denial, unrequited love were the themes. One of the most touching voices is that of Hatibullah Sultana, the sister of Mahmud II, who, as a result of political differences with her brother, was banished to a *yali* (seaside villa) on the Bosphorus. Her last poem, "The Song of Death," is a prophetic and visionary verse that alludes to poison and gives the impression that she herself had already chosen her own end: "The River [Bosphorus] is bitter to those who drink its water," she wrote.

There is an anonymous poem carved into the wall of the harem dungeon, written by a lamenting odalisque who was imprisoned for stealing a cheap mirror. She turned her tears into verse:

> *For a two-bit*
> *Mirror lost,*
> *This sitting here is caught*
> *By the men of the century.*

Zehra and I, 1953

Many of the women poets shared their gift with their sons. This may explain the fact that out of thirty-four sultans, eleven were distinguished poets.

There was a poem my grandmother often recited, with tears in her eyes and a quivering in her voice. From listening to her, I learned the Old Turkish words that were strange to a child, but I heard them so many times that I still know the poem by heart. It evokes the image of a lonely young odalisque who sits behind the lattices, through which she can barely discern the horizon beyond the Bosphorus; she recalls a memory hidden beyond the faraway Caucaus mountains:

Felek hüsnün diyarinda,	*Fate, in the land of love,*
Cüda kuldu bizi shimdi.	*Separates us now.*
Aramizda yüce dağlar,	*Mighty mountains between us,*
Iraktan merhaba shimdi.	*Hello from faraway now.*

Zehra, shortly after she was widowed, with her sons Sadri— my father (left)—and Aladdin.

Prayer

Women performed ablutions—washing face, feet, hands, and arms up to the elbows—before prayer. They covered their heads and laid a special prayer rug on the floor. They began prayer by pressing the open palms of their hands over face and eyes, shutting out all evil. Then they made an initial bow toward the East, the direction of Mecca, and began the sequence of bending, kneeling, touching the forehead to the ground, and resting back on the heels while their lips moved in silent recitation. Knees, hands, feet, nose, and forehead must touch the ground during prayer; it is a physical as well as a spiritual exercise: while the prayer purifies the soul, it also keeps the body healthy—much like yoga.

Secrets of Flowers and Birds

In John Frederick Lewis's painting *An Intercepted Correspondence,* we see a woman caught with a bouquet of flowers. Her act creates a commotion, since each flower had a symbolic meaning, signifying an illicit message from a secret lover. Lady Mary Wortley Montagu was intrigued with this form of communication in harems and popularized it in England, where it spread like an epidemic. Several books were published deciphering the secret held in each flower, the healing power of each, and how to communicate to your lover through flowers. English ladies quickly adopted the prescribed techniques to aid their own amorous encounters.

The Seraglio also had an impressive menagerie. Children loved playing in the Elephant House, which was filled with lions, tigers, leopards, and all sorts of other wild beasts, including, of course, elephants. The sultans gave their wives and odalisques monkeys, storks, exotic birds, and gazelles. Indeed, for the seventeenth-century transcendental poets Nedim, Baki, and others, "gazelle" became a metaphor for a beautiful girl. The gardens boasted coveys of nightingales, canaries, and doves. Colorful parrots and macaws cackled secrets from the private rooms. Abdulhamid II was obsessed with parrots, believing the birds could warn him of evil forces threatening his household. In his Yildiz Palace (Palace of the Stars), cages of different bird species filled each room and peacocks wandered the gardens of the sultans, like fantastic watchdogs, intimidating unwanted visitors.

Flowers and birds were often a source of inspiration for fables. Of all the birds, nightingales were most precious: Even in a golden cage, the nightingale yearns for its native land, says an old proverb. It is not difficult

to imagine that the nightingale in this eighteenth-century minstrel story may be a prince imprisoned in the Cage:

> *Once a nightingale loved a rose, and the rose, aroused by its song, woke trembling on her stem. It was a white rose, like all the roses at that time— white, innocent and virginal. It listened to the song, and something in its rose heart stirred. Then the nightingale came ever so near the trembling rose and whispered words that the rose could not help hearing. "Ben seviyorum seni gül, gül." "I love you rose, rose." At those words, the little heart of the rose blushed, and in that instant, pink roses were born. The nightingale came closer and closer, and though Allah, when he created the world, meant that the rose alone should never know earthly love, the rose opened its petals and the*

John Frederick Lewis, An Intercepted Correspondence, Cairo, 1869, Oil on panel, 29¼ x 34⅜ in., Photograph © 1985 Sotheby's Inc. An odalisque is caught with a bouquet, each flower part of a secret message from an illicit lover.

nightingale stole its virginity. In the morning, the rose in its shame turned red, giving birth to red roses; and although ever since then the nightingale comes nightly to ask for divine love, the rose refuses, for Allah never meant rose and bird to mate. The rose trembles at the voice of the nightingale but its petals remain closed.

Opium

Opium was distilled from the white poppy, the best of its kind, which grew abundantly in Asia Minor. In its simplest form, it was a black putty sometimes mixed with hashish and spices. More elaborate versions added ambergris, musk, and other essences. For important people in the palace, opium was concocted into a jewelry paste, with pulverized pearls, lapis lazuli, rubies, and emeralds. The sultan's opium pills, of course, were gilded, possibly the origin of the phrase, *altinilaci*—gilding the pill—the Turkish equivalent of gilding the lily.

Originally used as medicine, opium produced effects too pleasant to forget. It was most compatible with a sedentary and isolated life-style. Many sultans and their women began using it for pleasure.

The nights in the harem swelled with *keyf* (ultimate fulfillment) induced by opium pills and the drowsy peace of sated senses. The women indulged in drawn-out opium rituals, spending the evenings inhaling hookahs or eating opium, the "elixir of the night," dreaming of faraway lands beyond the latticed windows. Mostly, they preferred eating, rather than smoking opium because the effect lasted longer, dreams lingering until the rising of the sun. Amnesia followed; night after night of this induced chronic insomnia. The women began forgetting their distant homes, their lives before the Seraglio. In order to remember, they told stories to one another. A thousand stories of faraway lands, stories told in the night. At first it was a thousand nights of stories, but even numbers brought bad luck, so they added one.

*Eugène Delacroix,
Odalisque, 1845,
Oil on canvas,
14⅞ x 18¼ in.,
Fitzwilliam Museum,
Cambridge, England*

Song and Dance

The Hünkâr Sofasi (Hall of the Sultan) is the most spacious and elegant room in the harem, long and rectangular. At one end is a raised platform over which hangs a balcony. In this room, the sultans received their harem for pleasure and entertainment. One can imagine Selim III sitting on a throne under a baldachin, dressed in scarlet robes edged with sable. A dagger at his waist is studded with diamonds, a white aigrette in his turban holds in place a cluster of emeralds and rubies, and his bejewelled *nargileh* (waterpipe) is at his side. Before the throne is a carpet embroidered by the harem women. The valide sultana, kadins, and favorites recline on magnificent cushions. A group of odalisques, prohibited from sitting in the presence of the sultan, lean motionless against the wall. The beauty of these women, their exquisite silk and satin costumes enhanced with the most precious jewelry, the opulence of the furniture, all rival the wildest exaggerations of the *One Thousand and One Nights.*

Here, in the Hall of the Sultan, *sazende* (female musicians) performed on the balcony, while *chengis* (dancing girls) swayed before their lord. They wore low-necked muslin blouses, velvet vests, and voluminous skirts that opened like fans as they whirled around. They always performed in groups of twelve: the leader, ten dancers, and an apprentice. And the performance always ended with the dancers trying to reach a crystal ball suspended from the ceiling next to the throne. The sultan gave gifts to the girls who succeeded.

Selim III was a very fine musician and poet. During his reign (1789–1807) French dancing-masters and musicians were allowed into the outer courts of the harem to teach the girls—novices who had not yet converted to Islam—how to dance. When love affairs began flaring up between the odalisques and their music teachers, the sultans made sure the girls were never left alone with them; they studied in groups, chaperoned by eunuchs.

Sometimes male actors and mimes were invited to perform for the women—always carefully blindfolded, however. *The Wilder Shores of Love* (1954), a fictionalized biographical collection by Lesley Blanch, contains a story about the Debureau family (the subject of Marcel Carné's 1945 classic film *Children of Paradise*) performing in the harem:

> In 1810, the Debureau family, a Paris troup famous for their thrilling acrobatic and pantomime acts, was invited to appear before the Sultan. What transpired was a rather peculiar form of theatre: They were ushered through the sumptuous halls into a mirrored pavilion. Absolute silence reigned: it was completely deserted. . . . The acrobats were mystified. How could they divine that from behind slits in a brocaded curtain the Harem elite were watching? As they hesitated, a turbaned negro motioned them to begin their act. In silence, they spread out their threadbare strip of druggeting, pitiable against the Seraglio's Persian carpets. They went through their act, proceeding to its

Hünkar Sofasi, the Hall of the Sultan, where the harem women entertained the sultans

Mukaddes (dancer on the right) and Muazzez (sitting on her right) with women friends in the courtyard of their house

Three sazende
(female musicians),
ca. 1890

climax, a human pyramid. Father stood on uncle, brother supported cousin. Greatly daring, the young Debureau topped the whole swaying edifice, balanced on a ladder. . . . From the summit, Debureau could look down over the curtain, into the forbidden paradise below. Here the Sultan's ladies were gathered, "the voluptuous odalisques of the Seraglio, whose very regard could lead to death." His eyes met those of an unveiled odalisque. Overcome, he crashed to the ground, bringing the whole performance to an ignoble finish.

Shadow Puppets

Shadow world loved shadow plays. *Karagöz* was an extremely popular shadow-puppet show, full of robustly lewd antics handed down from one generation to another, surviving well into the twentieth century. It is described in Sadri Esat Siyavuşgil's *Karagöz* (1954):

> *The small screen of thin transparent cloth, hung about with handsome carpets to further conceal from us the mysterious puppet world behind it; illuminated but motionless, and adorned only with a large picture exquisitely cut and*

brilliantly colored. Sometimes this picture depicted a galley whose oars, illuminated by the flickering candlelight, created an illusion of movement; sometimes it would be a basket of flowers in a design so stylized as to evoke an admiring thrill from any abstractionist artist; and again, it might be a marvelous and incredible seraglio, tottering and fit to collapse at the first passionate sigh of its odalisques, or burst of rage from its eunuchs.

Karagoz plays were satirical shows with stock characters, often political. The play entitled *The Great Marriage,* for example, is a parody of arranged marriages in which the engaged couple do not see each other until the wedding night. The play ridicules this custom, which frequently caused a catastrophic row the day after. Chelebi has the laudable intention of marrying off his brother, the town drunkard, to make him give up his vice. Chelebi brings in Karagoz—always an abrasive male character—to play the role of the bride. A traditional wedding takes place, and the drunkard finds himself united in matrimony with a bearded creature. Confronted by this unappealing prospect, he promises to renounce his vice if the nightmare will only end.

Shopping

In the nineteenth century, women were allowed to drive in their *arabas* (carriages) through the city to the *bazaars* (markets). The araba would arrive at the gates of the market, where merchants displayed fabrics, scarves, ribbons, and slippers. Occasionally, peddlers brought such commodities in large bundles to the Seraglio, where the eunuchs greeted them at the gate, checked the bundles, and presented the goods to the women inside. Fabrics purchased were immediately sent to the palace tailor or dressmaker, who kept a record of everyone's measurements. Sometimes, female merchants, mostly Jewish women, were allowed inside the private apartments, bringing not only goods but also gossip from the outside. It was not uncommon for Christian merchants to marry Jewish women so that they could corner the harem market. These "bundle women" often became intermediaries for clandestine affairs and palace intrigue.

Excursions, Visits, and Outings

During the reign of Mahmud II (1808-39), a breath of "liberalism" stirred in the air. His mother was Nakshedil Sultana, the legendary Aimée de Rivery, a French girl from Martinique (and cousin to Josephine Bonaparte) who had been kidnapped by Levantine pirates on her way to convent school in France and eventually sold to the harem of Sultan Abdul Hamid I. Aimée made the best of her unexpected destiny, slowly endearing herself to the sultan and eventually becoming the valide sultana. During her reign, French culture insinuated itself into the harem. These were the times of midnight pleasures on the Bosphorus, times of music and dance.

Women like Aimée helped loosen social structures in the harem, allowing for considerably more freedom. Although heavily guarded by their eunuchs, the women were allowed to picnic at the Sweet Waters of Asia or

Harem women on an excursion in an araba *(carriage)*

Europe, two of the lovely estuaries opening into the Bosphorus. In a Preziosi painting we glimpse the fountain in the Sweet Waters, built by the queen mother Aimée de Rivery herself.

The Sweet Waters of Europe was a vast, grassy field along the confluence of the two streams that form the Golden Horn. There, in the shade of walnuts, terebinths, palm trees, and sycamores that make a succession of leafy pavilions, harem women gathered in circular groups, surrounded by their slaves, eunuchs, and children. Many pavilions and kiosks built by the sultans to entertain their harems became favorite flirting grounds for the aristocracy.

The women took kayiks along the stream for pleasure trips down the Bosphorus to the Sweet Waters of Asia, the meadow surrounding the Küçüksu (Little Water) stream, which flows into the Bosphorus on the Asian side of Constantinople. Like the Sweet Waters of Europe, it was a popular resort full of lovely *yalis* (seaside villas). In the meadow, people gathered to enjoy the fresh air, and lavish picnics included roast lamb cooked on spits over an open fire, corn-on-the-cob boiled in enormous black iron cauldrons, acrobats, puppet shows, and dancing bears, gypsy fortune tellers, Bulgarian shepherds playing on their pipes—all amid a field of tulips and hyacinths, gently swaying to the rhythm of the wind.

Such pleasure trips made the harem come alive with excitement. When the day for an outing arrived, the secretary made the announcement and the harem began to reverberate with activity. The women, all dressed in the same color—as required—left in carriages with drawn curtains. They brought along beautiful pitchers inlaid with gems and filled with sherbets to quench their thirst, and *chanta* (velvet bags embroidered with gold or silver) containing handkerchiefs, *bahshish* (tip money), alms for beggars, and hand mirrors to use in adjusting their veils. Eunuchs on horseback led the entourage and drew up ranks on both sides of the procession. The most important women occupied the forward and rear carriages, with novices riding in the middle.

Occasionally, the women, accompanied by the ever-present eunuchs, took rides into the country, stopping by cool streams to refresh themselves. Popular minstrels and dancers entertained them, but, of course, a curtain always separated the performers from their audience. Sometimes the procession stopped at one of the kiosks in Sweet Waters or other resorts, where the women would rest, recite their afternoon prayers, or sit in a gazebo eating fruit from the gardens and yogurt made by famous yogurt makers.

When they returned to the palace, they shared stories of their adventures with the girls who had stayed behind. They spun yarns about what they had eaten and whom they had seen, often gossiping about things that had not happened but that nevertheless added romance to their lives.

In *Haremin İçyüzü* (1936), Leyla Saz, poet, musician, and harem woman (1850–1936), describes an exquisite outing adventure in an interview recorded on the last day of her life.

How did you entertain yourself when you were young?
Music.

And dance?

In the palace, we also danced. Prince Murad played the piano and his sister and I would dance the polka. But our real joy was the simplicity of nature. We

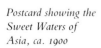

*Amadeo Count
Preziosi,* The
Sweet Waters
of Europe, *ca. 1845,
Watercolor on paper,
Private collection*

*Postcard showing the
Sweet Waters of
Asia, ca. 1900*

would run away from the noise of the city and throw ourselves into the water under the moon . . . Sweet Waters of Asia, Sweet Waters of Europe. Between Bebek and Emirgan [two small towns on the Bosphorus], there were hundreds of kayiks [row boats] and women in silk and diaphanous veils like apparitions. I can never forget those beautiful days. The crystal voices [of the singers] licked the shores of the Bosphorus, trembling and dying into the water. We hid our emotions even from the moon, closed our eyes, and went into a reverie. The dawn found us like this.

Painted and gilded kayiks were luxurious boats with brocaded cushions, Oriental rugs, or velvet carpets richly embroidered in silver or gold, crimson or purple. They rowed up and down the Bosphorus, escorted by a sparkling shoal of jeweled fish ornaments, *hirame,* attached to the boats by chains, trailing from the stern and out over the surface of the water in a fan of splendor.

Festivals and Special Days

On the Persian New Year, celebrated during the spring solstice (March 21), the grand vizier and other important ministers presented gifts to the sultan. In the harem, the women offered their own felicitations and received gifts.

In 1554, a Dutch envoy who visited Istanbul brought back to Holland something that would change the nature of its national identity. Ogier Busbecq stumbled upon a secret on the shores of the Sweet Waters of Asia, a field of strange flowers. He had never seen anything like it before, and when he expressed his awe, someone presented him with a sack of bulbs. These he planted that autumn on the flats near his home in Holland, and in the early spring, tulips of all colors sprouted. People came from all over to see and were enchanted. Tulipomania spread throughout the Netherlands, almost leading the nation to bankruptcy. Carriages full of bulbs left Istanbul in 1562, arriving at their destination months later. This tradition continues to this day. Every summer a carriage loaded with bulbs of all varieties treks from Istanbul to Holland—though, over the years, the Dutch have developed their own hybrids. The name of the flower is a derivative from the Turkish nickname for it, *tulbend,* meaning turban.

Istanbul was seized with its own tulipomania years later, during the early eighteenth century. In fact, this era of Ottoman history is known as the Reign of the Tulip, when Sultan Ahmed III, who reigned from 1703 to 1730, shunned war and concentrated on cultural matters, building summer palaces along the Sweet Waters designed in Iranian and European architectural styles. Beds of tulips and myriad other flowers decorated gardens in a riot of color. Istanbul glowed, and entertainments of incredible splendor took place, inspiring great literature and raising to a new level of perfection the miniature painting for which Ottoman artists of this period are celebrated. Jean-Claude Flachat gives a colorful account of a tulip fête in *Observations sur le commerce* (1766):

> *It takes place in April. Wooden galleries are erected in the courtyard of the New Palace. Vases of tulips are placed on either side of these rows in the form of an amphitheater. Torches and, from the topmost shelves, cages of canaries hang, with glass balls full of colored water, alternating with the flowers. The reverberation of the light is as lovely a spectacle in the daytime as at night. The wooden structures around the courtyard, arbors, towers and pyramids are beautifully decorated and a feast to the eye.*
>
> *Art creates illusion, harmony brings this lovely place to life, enabling one to reach the mirage of one's own dreams.*
>
> *The Sultan's kiosk is in the center, and here the gifts sent by the palace dignitaries are on display. The source of their origin is explained to His Highness. It is an opportunity to see eagerness to please. Ambition and rivalry strive to create something new. What may be lacking in originality is replaced with magnificence and richness.*
>
> *On several occasions, the chief eunuch has described to me how the women display all their skills on such festive occasions as this, in order to obtain something they desire or to entertain everyone. . . . Each strives to distinguish herself. They are full of charms, each with the same objective. . . . One has never seen elsewhere to what lengths the resources of the intellect can go with women who want to seduce a man through vanity. The graceful dancing, melodic voices, harmonious music, elegant costumes, witty conversation, the ecstasies, the femininity and love—the most voluptuous, I might add that the most artful of coquetries of lust are displayed here.*

Disenchantment

During the late nineteenth century, with the ascension of Abdul Hamid II, the music ended and the frolicking stopped. Beset with paranoid fears of assassination, the sultan banned all gatherings, including musical performances, boat trips, and dances. His reign became a period of social mourning. In *Turkey Today* (1908), Grace Ellison records one woman's response to this sad development. Halide Edip's words (1914) speak of the pall that must have descended over all harems, deprived of the distractions that made the life of a captive bearable:

> *We are idle and useless and therefore, very unhappy. Women are sorely needed everywhere; there is work that we can all do, but the customs of the country will not allow us to do it.*
>
> *Had we possessed the blind fatalism of our grandmothers, we would probably suffer less, but with culture, as so often happens, we began to doubt the wisdom of the faith which would have been our consolation. We analyzed our life and discovered nothing but injustice and cruelty, unnecessary sorrow. Resignation and culture cannot go together.*

Zeyneb Hanim, who inspired Djénane, heroine of Pierre Loti's harem novel, The Disenchanted

How can I impress upon you the anguish of our everyday life—our continual haunting dread? No one can imagine the sorrow of a Turkish woman's life but those who, like ourselves, have led this life. Sorrow indeed belongs to Turkish women, they have bought the exclusive rights with their very souls. Could the history of any country be more terrible than the reign we are living? You will say I am morbid; perhaps I am, but how can it be otherwise when the best years of my life have been poisoned?

You ask how we spend the day! Dreaming, principally. What else can we do? The view of the Bosphorus with the ships coming and going is the consolation to us captives. The ships to us are fairy godmothers who will take us away one day, somewhere we know not—but we gaze at the beautiful Bosphorus through the latticed windows and thank Allah for at least this pleasure in life.

Unlike most harem women, I write. . . . This correspondence is the dream side of my existence and in moments of extra despair and revolt, for we are always unhappy, I take refuge in this correspondence addressed to no one in particular. And yet in writing, I risk my life. What do I care?

Listen to this: How I hate Western education and culture for the suffering it has brought me! Why should I have been born in a harem rather than one of those free Europeans about whom I read? Why should fate have chosen certain persons rather than others for this eternal suffering?

Sometimes we sing, accompanying our Eastern music on the Turkish lute. But our songs are all in the minor key, our landscapes are all blotted out in sadness and sometimes the futility and unending sorrow of our lives rise up and choke us and cause the tears to flow, but often our life is too soul-crushing even for tears and nothing but death can alter this.

Like a true daughter of my race, I start the day with "good resolutions." I will do something to show that I have at least counted the hours as they drag themselves past! Night comes, my dadi [old nurse] comes to undress me and braid up my hair. . . . I tumble onto my divan and am soon fast asleep, worn out with the exertion I have not even made.

Ayhan, posing in a traditional wedding dress of red velvet embroidered with gold

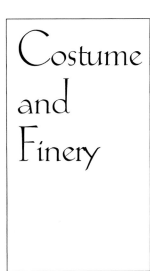

Costume and Finery

*A thousand nymphs with many a sprightly glance·
Form'd round the radiant wheels an airy dance · Celestial
shapes! in fluid light array'd · Like twinkling stars their
beamy sandals play'd; · Their lucid mantles glitter'd in
the sun, · (Webs half so bright the silkworm never spun)·
Transparent robes, that bore the rainbow's hue, · And
finer than the nets of pearly dew · That morning spreads
o'er every opening flower.—Sir William (Oriental)
Jones,* The Seven Fountains *(1772)*

Throughout the centuries, the harem was like a grand stage set, with the players performing in an extravagant costume drama. The sixteenth-century *Kanun-name* (Book of Laws) detailed the rules governing the customs and formalities of court ceremony, dress, and etiquette. The color and design of court attire, from headdress down to shoes, differentiated the members of the royal household according to rank and duty. Each ceremony was an occasion for displaying the most splendid costumes in the world. The sultan never saw a woman wearing the same dress more than once.

From the rare personal accounts by harem women, from reports of those who stole glimpses of the harem, from the description of one who befriended a eunuch, and from the marketplace gossip of the clothes dealers and vendors, we learn of rich gold and silver brocades, of fine satins and tricolored cloth, of velvets, silks, extraordinary jewels, and accessories. Lady Mary Wortley Montagu described in 1717:

> *a girdle as broad as the broadest English ribbon, entirely covered with
> diamonds. Round her neck she wore three chains which reached to her knees;
> one of large pearls, at the bottom of which hung a fine colored emerald as big as
> a turkey egg; another consisting of two hundred emeralds closely joined . . .
> every one as large as a half-crown piece. . . . But her earrings eclipsed all the
> rest. They were two diamonds, shaped exactly like pears, as large as a big
> hazel nut. . . . She had four strings of pearls, the whitest and most perfect in
> the world, at least enough to make four necklaces, every one as large as the
> Duchess of Marlborough's.*

Lady Montagu also wrote of large diamond bracelets, a gigantic ruby surrounded by twenty drops of clear diamond, and a headdress covered with "bodkins of emeralds and diamonds." This dazzling extravaganza cul-

*Charles Amadee
Phillippe Van Loo,*
A Sultana Dressing
or Marquise
Pompadour in
Turkey, *1774,
Oil on canvas, 10 ft.
6 in. x 12 ft. 5⅝ in.,
Musée du Louvre,
Paris*

minated in "five rings . . . the largest I ever saw in my life. It is for jewelers
to compute the value of these things . . . but I am sure that no European
Queen has half the quantity."

Bassano da Zara, in *I Costumi et i modi particolari de la vita de Turchi*
(1545), describes women dressed richly in silk, with lined cloaks sweeping
to the ground and laced-up boots fitting tight to the ankle. All had trousers
and chemises of very fine linen or muslin, some white and some dyed red,
yellow, or blue. On their heads they wore small round caps embroidered
with satin, damask, or silk, and, under these, colored strips of thin silk as
wide as a priest's stole, with a little fringe at the edges. Some preferred caps
of velvet or brocade, to which a stole was attached. Some wore two caps, a
small white one with another of silk on top. In a 1599 account contained in
Early Voyages and Travels in the Levant, Thomas Dallam recalled the sight of
thirty concubines spied through a grate in the harem wall:

> *Theie wore upon theire heads nothinge bute a little capp of clothe of goulde,
> which did but cover the crowne of her heade; no bandes a boute their neckes,
> nor anthinge but faire cheans of pearle and a juell hanginge on their breste, and*

juels in their ears; their coats were like a souldier's mandilyon [a buttoned cloak], some of reed sattan and som of blew, and some of other collors, and girded like a lace of contraire collor; they wore britchis of scamatie, fine clothe made of coton woll, as whyte as snow and as fine as lane [muslin], for I could desarne the skin of their thies throughe it. These britchis cam doone to their mydlege; som of them did weare fine cordevan buskins, and som had their legs naked, with a goulde ringe on the smale of her legg; on her foute a velvett panttoble [shoe] 4 or 5 inches hie. I stood so longe loukinge upon them that he which had showed me all this kindnes began to be verrie angrie with me. He made a wrye mouthe, and stamped with his foute to make me give over looking; the which I was verrie lothe to dow, for that sighte did please me wondrous well.

In the seclusion of the harem, women wore beautiful and elaborate clothes combined with exquisite accessories that produced masterpieces of grace and charm. In a letter to her sister, Lady Mar, dated April 1, 1717, Lady Montagu writes of the clothes she herself wore when visiting the women of the sultan's harem:

The first piece of my dress is a pair of drawers, very full, that reach to my shoes, and conceal the legs more modestly than your petticoats. They are of a rose-coloured damask, brocaded with silver flowers. My shoes are of white kid

Left:
*Théodore Leblanc,
Haroufah, Muslim
Bride, 1835,
Bibliothèque
Nationale, Paris*

Right:
*"Fiancée Druze."
Bonfils Studio,
Lebanon, 1870–80,
Musée de l'Homme,
Paris.* The tantur
headdress, made of
silvered copper, was
worn by betrothed
and married Druze
women in nineteenth-
century Lebanon
and Syria.

leather, embroidered with gold. Over this hangs my smock, of a fine white silk gauze, edged with embroidery. This smock has wide sleeves, hanging half way down the arm, and is closed at the neck with a diamond button; but the shape and colour of the bosom very well to be distinguished through it. The antery is a waistcoat, made close to the shape, of white and gold fringe, and should have diamond or pearl buttons. My caftan, of the same stuff with my drawers, is a robe exactly fitted to my shape, and reaching to my feet, with very long straight falling sleeves. Over this is the girdle, of about four fingers broad which all that can afford have entirely of diamonds or other precious stones; those who will not be at that expense have it of exquisite embroidery on satin; but it must be fastened before with a clasp of diamonds. The curdee is a loose robe they throw off or put on according to the weather, being of a rich brocade (mine is green and gold), either lined with ermine or sables; the sleeves reach very little below the shoulders. The headdress is composed of a cap, called kalpock which is in winter of fine velvet embroidered with pearls or diamonds, and in summer of a light shining silver stuff. This is fixed on one side of the head, hanging a little way down with a gold tassel, and bound on, either with a circle of diamonds or a rich embroidered handkerchief. On the other side of the head, the hair is laid flat; and here the ladies are at liberty to show their fancies; some putting flowers, others a plume of heron's feathers, and in short, what they please; but the most general fashion is a large bouquet of jewels,

Nineteenth-century studio photograph of harem women

made like natural flowers; that is, the buds of pearl; the rose, of different coloured rubies; the jessamines, of diamonds; the jonquils, of topazes, etc., so well set and enamelled, 'tis hard to imagine anything of that kind so beautiful. The hair hangs at its full length behind, divided into tresses braided with pearl or ribbon, which is always in great quantity.

In a letter written on March 9, 1850, from Egypt, Florence Nightingale relates a visit to a far more humble harem:

Oh! what a curious sight it was—the incongruities!—the principal lady, the married sister, dressed like an Oriental queen, but without a shift or anything which could be washed, next to her skin, and sitting upon the mud floor—no furniture but a slave—and the square holes for windows stuffed with mats. The mother was baking downstairs; and two slave wives peeked in at the door. I never saw anything so beautiful, so really beautiful, as the woman's dress— of course it was her only one:—Cachmire trousers, of a delicate small pattern, —a yelek, with hanging sleeves of exquisite Bursa silk, crimson and white, trimmed with gold binding,—a tob, with immense sleeves of lilac silk,—and over it (for the Arab never wears her gayest clothes outside) a purple gauze drapery embroidered with silver, and veil of same color, embroidered in silks; and withal she had the carriage of an empress.

"Jeune princesse sortant du bain": nineteenth-century studio photograph of an Egyptian princess

The extravagant beauty of the women in the harem and their elaborate costumes were concealed in public, where they dressed with uniform drabness. On a rare boat trip to the Sweet Waters or on a shopping excursion to the Grand Bazaar, harem women became ghosts of their former beauty, dressed in the *feradge,* a long, square tunic with loose sleeves, hanging nearly to the ground, like a shapeless black cape, falling from the shoulders to the feet, concealing everything. Rich women and members of the royal harem wore silk *feradges* in pink or lilac, with a lining of black or white satin and ornamentation of tassels, braiding, and velvet edging.

Outdoors they always wore the veil. The Renaissance traveler Bassano da Zara described it in his 1545 *I Costumi et i modi particolari de la vita de Turchi:*

> *They wear a towel (a cloth or woolen underscarf) round the neck and head, so that one can only see their eyes and mouth, and these they cover with a thin silk scarf a palm's width each way, through which they can see and not be seen by others. The scarf is fastened with three pins to a suitable part of the head above the forehead, so that when they go through the streets and meet other women, they raise the scarf that hangs over their faces and kiss one another.*

Opposite left:
A woman wearing a yashmak

Opposite right:
A family member wearing a yashmak *and carrying a* chanta

Left:
A Turkish noblewoman in nineteenth-century costume

Right:
A woman wearing a feradge

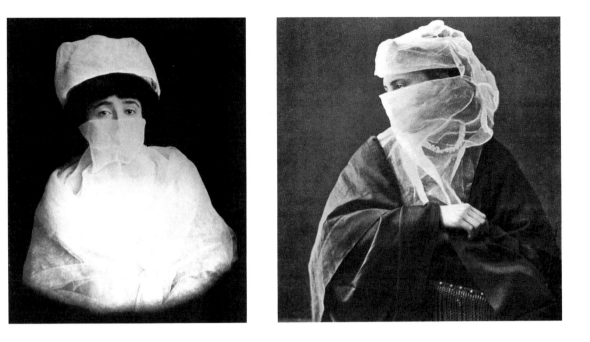

By tradition the veil signifies *harem,* sanctuary—still a powerful taboo. The Koran enjoins women believers to cover their faces and bodies from men, in order to prevent temptation. Gradually, the "Passing of the Veil" became an institution, marking the rite of passage from girlhood to womanhood and representing protection of virtue. As soon as a girl first menstruated, her face was veiled, her hands gloved. From that point on, no man, except her close male relatives, was allowed to see her countenance. In traditional Islamic cultures, most women would sooner stand naked in a marketplace than uncover their faces. For the face is inviolate.

As only the eyes are visible above the veil, immense meaning has to be conveyed by a mere glance. In Rama Mehta's 1977 novel, *Inside the Haveli,* we learn that wearing a veil did have advantages. It allowed the wearer "to think while others talked. To her delight, she had discovered that through her thin muslin sari, she could see everyone and yet not be seen by them." Traditionally, in most villages, women did not wear veils; the entire village was considered an extended family. Even nowadays, while women work unveiled with men in the fields, as soon as they see a stranger from another village, they pull down their scarves to hide their faces.

After the conquest of Constantinople in 1453, ladies of the harem insisted on a modification of their costume and obtained permission to wear the *yashmak* of the Byzantine women instead of the linen mask with two holes for the eyes. The yashmak was a diaphanous veil exclusive to Istanbul, made of two pieces of fine muslin or, in the nineteenth century, tarlatan, which was folded across or left as a single thickness. One piece was bound around the head like a bandage, over the forehead down to the eyebrows, knotted just above the nape of the neck and left to fall over the back, reaching to the waist. The other covered the lower part of the face and was tied together in such a way with the first as to give the illusion of a single veil. It was either tucked in underneath the *feradge* or attached to the other piece at the nape of the neck. The translucency partially and tantalizingly revealed the facial features behind it. However, a woman was extremely careful not to expose the nose, lest she be taken for an infidel or a prostitute.

The seventeenth-century Turkish writer Sinan Chelebi recorded this jewellike vignette in his *Saadabad:*

> *Two beauties, one in lemon yellow, the other in pink, were going towards the green meadow in their glittering picnic carriages. Their yashmaks were crystal clear, their cheeks like roses, their necks like silver, their hair like hyacinths. They were not afraid of the evil eye falling on them as they moved in tiny steps like beautiful doves in their chedik shoes.*

The *cedik,* or *chedik,* was a shoe or slipper-boot for strolling in the garden; it was high in front, usually made of yellow Moroccan leather but sometimes made of velvet or other soft fabrics.

Mohammed considered beautiful hands the most seductive part of a woman's body. To compensate for being almost completely shrouded, women made maximum use of their hands and their eyes, their only visible assets. With a subtle gesture they could speak a thousand words. During the nineteenth century, the "jealous Turks" added a final touch to the veiling of their women—gloves—thereby hiding the final vestige of flesh, save the eyes.

Sunshades, parasols, and fans offered protection not only from the elements but also from the curious glances of strangers. Parasols had lace tops, beads, and flowers; some featured ribs of gold studded with sapphires. Fans were made of peacock or ostrich feathers and adorned with diamonds, rubies, and emeralds, their handles of tortoiseshell, ivory, or mother-of-pearl. The indoor fan, which every guest room offered, was made of date leaves with an ivory handle.

The *mendil* (handkerchief) had a special place in the hearts of harem women. Fruits and gifts were wrapped in them, and stories were told of handkerchiefs "filled with Turkish delight" and furtively passed to strangers or fantasy lovers. The color of the handkerchief, too, always conveyed an unspoken message:

red	*passionate love*
orange	*heartache*
green	*intention*
pink	*love bond*
purple	*suffering from love*
black	*hopelessness, separation*
blue	*hope for union*

A handkerchief that was torn and burned signified, "I am dying of heartache—fading and wilting."

"When I first came here, I did not quite understand what the attraction could be about the mystery with which the more interesting half of the people of the Orient enshrouds itself," the French writer Gérard de Nerval wrote in *Voyage en Orient* (1843–51). "But a few days sufficed to show me that a woman who knows herself to be the object of attention can usually find an opportunity to let herself be seen—if she is beautiful."

For a woman untethered to a eunuch or skilled in the ways of eluding one, the drabness of her attire had a redeeming value. It made one woman indistinguishable from another; and for a man to approach or talk with a woman on the street was unthinkable, since her veil and cloak were as sacred as the doors of the harem. A husband could not tell his wife apart from all the rest of the montonous dark figures. Even under suspicion, there was no way of confirming a woman's identity. Thus, she could take advantage of her anonymity to slip away for a clandestine meeting with her lover—often on her way to the baths. Gérard de Nerval observed:

As for freedom to go out and pay calls, a woman of free birth undoubtedly possesses it. The husband's right in this matter is limited to sending slaves to accompany her, but as a precaution, that is of little consequence, for it would be perfectly easy for the wives, either to buy the slaves over or else to go out in disguise, either from the bath or from one of their friends' houses, whilst the attendants were watching at the door. In reality, the mask and uniformity of dress would give them much greater freedom than Europeans, if they were inclined to go in for intrigues. The merry stories told at night in the cafes often deal with the adventures of lovers who disguise themselves as women so as to make their way into some harem.

The Baths

Forty days after a baby was born, his mother and the midwife took him to the baths for the first time for a special ceremony. The midwife broke a duck's egg inside a bowl and smeared it on the baby's face. This was so done that the child would have the ability to swim as well as a duck.—Musahipzade Celal, Eski Istanbul Yaşayisi *(19th century)*

Women of the harem were renowned for their luminous complexions and satin skin. To wash and purify was a religious obligation. It is not surprising, therefore, that so many baths were built in the Seraglio. The sultan, the valide, and the wives all had private baths, while the other women of the harem shared a large bathhouse, which sometimes welcomed the sultan as well.

The *hamam* (Turkish bath) is an adaptation of the Byzantine bath, which itself derived from Roman *thermae*. Many of the famous baths were renovated from the Byzantine originals. While thermae were concentrated in urban areas and fashionable resorts, hamams were scattered throughout the provinces. Until recently, Roman, or Pompeiian, aqueducts were used in the baths, distributing water under the floor or through numerous foundations. A central source often heated the two adjoining hamams, with the women's bath on one side and the men's on the other.

For harem women, deprived of so many freedoms, the hamam became an all-consuming passion and a most luxurious pastime. The bathing ritual took several hours, often lasting into the evening, as Julia Pardoe describes in her *Beauties of the Bosphorus* (1830): "The heavy, dense, sulphurous vapour that filled the place and almost suffocated me—the subdued laughter and whispered conversations of . . . [the slaves'] mistresses, murmuring along in an undercurrent of sound—the sight of nearly three hundred women, only partially dressed, and that in fine linen so perfectly saturated with vapour that it revealed the whole outline of the figure—the busy slaves passing and repassing, naked from the waist upwards, and with their arms folded upon their bosoms, balancing on their heads piles of fringed or embroidered napkins—groups of lovely girls, laughing, chatting, and refreshing themselves with sweetmeats, sherbet, and lemonade—parties of playful children, apparently quite indifferent to the dense atmosphere which made

Jean-Léon Gérôme, The Bath, ca. 1880–85, Oil on canvas, 29 x 23½ in., The Fine Arts Museums of San Francisco; Mildred Anna Williams Collection

me struggle for breath . . . all combined to form a picture like the illusory semblance of a phantasmagoria, almost leaving me in doubt whether that on which I looked were indeed reality, or the mere creation of a distempered brain."

When women came to call on women in other harems, they stayed for several days. Odalisques greeted and immediately escorted them to the baths to clean and refresh themselves. In her 1908 memoir, *Haremlik,* Demetra Vaka, a young Greek woman, returns to Istanbul after traveling abroad and visits her Turkish friends: "Slave women undressed us and took us to the bathing house on the shore of the sea. After the bath, we were put in loose, clean garments lent to us by the mistress."

An anonymous Italian work, *Constantinopoli e di Turchi* (1510), contains an engraving of ladies proceeding to the baths, followed by a train of slaves carrying on their heads magnificent bathing robes, towels, perfumes, and baskets full of the fruit and pastry their mistresses will consume during their long retreat at the bathhouse. For women living in harems, the bath provided a chance to go out into the world. For some, the pilgrimage afforded sufficient freedom to arrange clandestine meetings. For all, the public baths were a center for gossip and a wellspring of invented scandal. They were the women's private clubs.

At one time, the Seraglio had thirty or so baths, but today very few remain intact. Most have been torn down and converted into other rooms —the clues to their past found only in the perforated domes that signify the hamam. The two adjoining baths in the Seraglio, the sultan's and the valide sultana's, do survive—marble edifices with tall narrow columns and a skylight. Once, the floors and the walls were inlaid with the most opulent faience tiles; the water ran from brass faucets into large marble sinks, and women poured it over themselves out of bowls of silver and gold. No tubs were used because of a superstitious belief that still water contained *ifrits* (evil beings). (Indeed, the women were not permitted to recite verses from the Koran, since the baths were generally a favorite resort of ifrits and djinns.)

Mrs. Harvey, an English woman traveling in Turkey, found the baths less than soothing: "In an instant I felt as a shrimp, if he feels at all, must feel in boiling water—I was boiled," she wrote in her *Travels* (1871). "I looked at my companion; her face was a gorgeous scarlet. In our best Turkish and in faint and imploring accents, we gasped 'Take us away!' All in vain. We had to be boiled and rubbed and boiled and rubbed we must be."

A hundred years later, the operation had not changed—at least judging from Marianne Alireza's memoir, *At the Drop of a Veil* (1971): "I sat naked on the stool while steam swirled around me, the painted cherubs watched, and I was soaped and scrubbed raw with the shredded wheat biscuit, otherwise known as a loofa, a spongelike tropical gourd. After half drowning me with her pitiless bucket rinsings, Hayat finished the deluge with cologne and powder and was as soaked as I was."

Women ladled perfumed water over one another and hennaed their hair, hands, and feet. On special occasions, like weddings, floral designs made from henna were stamped on their bodies. In his *I Costumi et i modi particolari de la vita de Turchi,* Bassano da Zara details the use of henna:

> They are fond of black hair, and if any woman by nature does not possess it she acquires it by artificial means. If they are fair or grey through old age they use a red dye like that with which horses' tails are dyed. It's called Chnà [henna]. The same is used on their nails, sometimes whole hand, sometimes the foot following the shape of the shoe, and again some dye the pubic region and four fingers' length above it. And for this reason they remove their hairs, considering it a sin to have any in their private parts.

"Just as in the case of henna, which is a good preventative against perspiration," A. M. Penzer reports in *The Harem* (1936), "so certain forms of eye-black [kohl, surme, kajal, tutia, etc.] give coolness to the eyes and help to prevent opthalmalia, as well as being a guard against the evil eye. The meeting of the eyebrows, while considered beautiful in Mohammedan countries, is not liked among the Hindus, and in Iceland, Denmark, Germany, Greece, and Bohemia it is considered a sign of a werewolf or a vampire." The women also scrubbed their skin with pumice stone, washed their hair with egg yolks, and used egg whites to eliminate the crow's feet around the eyes. Each woman brought to the baths an assortment of perfumes, essences, and creamy concoctions. They experimented with these and traded beauty secrets.

"It is not altogether easy to define the beauty of the Turkish women," Edmondo de Amicis declared in his 1896 travelogue *Constantinople.* "In thinking of them, I may say I always see a very white face, two black eyes, a crimson mouth, and a sweet expression. But then, they almost all of them paint, whiten their skin with almond and jasmine paste, lengthen their eyebrows with India ink, color their eyelids, powder their necks, draw circles around their eyes and put patches on their cheeks; but in all these they employ taste and discretion, unlike the belles of Fez, who use whitewash brushes to beautify themselves with."

Spices such as cloves and ginger were used not simply in cooking and making potpourries, but were rubbed on the body because the women in harems believed that certain mixtures increased powers of seduction. The English explorer Samuel Baker described how a woman would make a hole in the ground, fill it with embers of sandalwood, frankincense, and myrrh, and crouch over the hole, her clothes arranged around her as a sort of tent to capture the fumes. This ritual perfumed the body and the clothes as well as warded off the evil eye. We see an exquisite recreation of this in the John Singer Sargent painting *Fumée d'Ambre Gris.*

Sometimes arguments arose among the women, culminating in clogs and bowls flying in the air. Sturdy bath attendants seized the culprits by the waist and threw them out into a cold courtyard to cool off. Those clogs—high-stilted wooden contraptions called *pattens*—were required footwear in the baths. Art objects, decorated with inlaid mother-of-pearl and other precious stones, pattens also preserved tender feet from the heated bath marble and reduced the danger of slipping on the wet floor. They kept the wearer well above the flowing water, protecting her skin from corrosive depilatories and other ungodly substances swirling around on the floor. They also prevented contamination by jealous djinns hiding in the secret and dark corners of the hamam.

It was considered a sin to have hair on one's private parts, and harem women, extremely observant on this point, scurried off to the hamams at the first sign of hair. They removed hair not only from their legs and underarms, but from all body crevices, even nostrils and ears. They spread themselves with a burning paste, which was later scraped off with the sharp edges of mussel shells. The paste, according to Jean Thevenot's *Travels into the Levant* (1656), "was made of a certain mineral called *rusma,* beat into a powder, and with lime and water made into a paste, which they apply to the parts where they would have their hair fetch't off, and in less than half a quarter of an hour, all the hair falls off with the paste, by throwing hot water upon it: They know when it is time to throw water by seeing if the hair comes off with the paste; for if it be left too long sticking on the place, after it had eaten off the hair, it would corrode the flesh." Rusma contained arsenic and could tarnish the flesh unless applied meticulously. The advantage of using a depilatory rather than a razor was that the paste removed the hair at the follicle, while shaving only leveled off the surface of the epidermis, and the hair grew back faster and stronger than before.

My grandmother introduced me to *ada,* which is still a popular form of depilatory in the provinces. This simple, candylike paste of lemon and sugar is difficult to bring to the right consistency. Two parts granulated beet sugar are caramelized and added to one part lemon juice, while stirring constantly over low heat until it begins to bubble. It is removed quickly from the heat and tested by dropping a tiny ball in a glass of water. If it crystallizes, the ada is done; if it dissolves, it needs to cook longer. When ready, it is puttied in cool hands and the desired amount is spread on the hairy part of the body. Then it is vigorously pulled off, bringing the hair with it.

After hours of being steamed, scrubbed, and massaged, the bathers moved to the *tepidarium,* a resting room where the sensual pleasure of bathing culminated in sweet exhaustion and relaxation. Tepidariums had private and public rooms. After passing through a vestibule and a series of warm rooms into the center, where a fountain of tepid water splashed, women were massaged, scraped, and pumiced. In an adjoining room, they were rinsed, left to rest on mattresses, given coffee, and told the latest stories. Beautiful gilded hangings, encrusted with pearls, decorated the walls. Heavy Persian rugs and low sofas, upholstered in gold and silver embroideries and piled high with cushions, completed the decor. The women took naps,

Husein Fazil Enderuni,
Women's Bath,
18th century,
Miniature from
Zanan-Name,
Istanbul University
Library

Jean-Léon Gérôme, The Great Bath at Bursa, ca. 1885, Photogravure, 9½ x 6½ in., Collection of the author. The waters of Bursa have long been renowned for their healing powers; the sultans built several beautiful hamams (baths) to take advantage of this.

groomed each other, smoked bejeweled *chibuks* (very long pipes), and nibbled on slices of melon or savored delicately perfumed sherbets. "When at length they venture into the outer hall," observed Julia Pardoe in her *Beauties of the Bosphorus*, "they at once spring upon their sofas, where the attentive slaves fold them in warm cloths, and pour essence upon their hair, which they twist loosely without attempting to dislodge the wet, and then cover with handsome headkerchiefs or embroidered muslin; perfumed water is scattered over the face and hands, and the exhausted bather sinks into a luxurious slumber beneath a coverlet of satin or of eider down. The centre of the floor, meanwhile, is like a fair; sweet-meat, sherbet, and fruit merchants parade up and down, hawking their wares. Negresses pass to and fro with the dinners or *chibuks* (pipes) of their several mistresses; secrets are whispered—confidences are made; and altogether, the scene is so strange, so new, and withal so attractive, that no European can fail to be both interested and amused by a visit to a Turkish Hammam."

The hamam was also the place where women could easily be observed

John Singer Sargent, Fumée d'Ambre Gris, 1880, Oil on canvas, 54¾ x 35¹¹/₁₆ in., Sterling and Francine Clark Art Institute, Williamstown, Massachusetts.

Jean-Auguste
Dominique Ingres,
The Turkish Bath,
1832, Oil on
canvas on wood,
diameter: 43¼ in.,
Musée du Louvre,
Paris

by outsiders, who were usually bedazzled, not shocked, by what they saw. Lady Montagu, writing in 1717, registers the strong homoerotic overtones:

> *The first sofas were covered with cushions and rich carpets, on which sat the ladies; and on the second, their slaves behind them, but without any distinction of rank by their dress, all being in the state of nature, that is, in plain English, stark naked, without any beauty or defect concealed. Yet there was not the least*

> *wanton smile or immodest gesture amongst them. They walked and moved with the same majestic grace which Milton describes of our general mother. There were many amongst them as exactly proportioned as ever any goddess was drawn by the pencil of Guido or Titian—and most of their skins shiningly white, only adorned by their beautiful hair divided into many tresses, hanging*

Paul-Louis Bouchard,
A Harem Beauty,
c. 1890, Oil on canvas,
84⅝ x 49¼ in.,
Private collection

on their shoulders, braided either with pearl or ribbon, perfectly representing the
figures of the Graces. . . . to see so many fine women naked, in different
postures, some in conversation, some working, others drinking coffee or sherbet,
and many negligently lying on their cushions, while their slaves (generally
pretty girls of seventeen or eighteen) were employed in braiding their hair in
several pretty fancies. In short, it is the women's coffee-house, where all the
news of the town is told, scandal invented, etc.

The hamams were also places where women examined each other, and the go-betweens had an eye feast. A sultan's sister describes a slave woman she intends to present to her mighty brother: "Her proportions were perfect. She had a body like crystal, arms like marrows, and narrow wrists. She had an indescribably fine complexion! Like fresh feta cheese or Turkish delight. And the color? Like roses. Forty-one *Mashallah* [God protect her]!"

The baths were not only a source of sensuous escape for women but also provided an erotic distraction for the harem masters. Jean-Claude Flachat, a French industrialist, describes how Sultan Mahmud I devised a game for his odalisques by concealing himself behind a secret window overlooking the baths and watching the arrival of the women. All the odalisques were given chemises to wear, but this devious master had had the stitches removed and the fabric lightly glued at the seams. He watched with amusement as the chemises peeled off the women's bodies when they came in contact with the steaming water.

Eroticism in the baths was not reserved for the master alone. For women who were bred in the ways of pleasure and who rarely attained the sultan's bed, it was a chance to feast their eyes on beautiful bodies and satisfy each other. While washing and massaging one another, while scrutinizing closely for the first signs of emerging hair, the women often became lovers as well as friends. Bassano da Zara reflects: "It is common knowledge that as a result of this familiarity in washing and massaging women fall very much in love with each other. And one often sees a woman in love with another one just like a man and woman. And I have known Greek and Turkish women, on seeing a lovely young girl, seek occasion to bathe with her just to see her naked and handle her."

Edmondo de Amicis makes a similar observation: "Women have the most ardent relationships with one another. They wear the same colors, same perfumes, put on patches of the same size and shape, and make enthusiastic demonstrations. One European woman traveller claims that all the vices of ancient Babylon exist among them."

Food

The dinner was set on a velvet cloth embroidered with silver threads. A silver tray was placed on a six-legged silver stand, decked with salads, caviar, olives, and cheeses. The salt, pepper, and cinnamon shakers were inlaid with precious gems. Lemon juice was served in a carved crystal pitcher. In the center was a silver trivet. Around the tray were delicately embroidered silk napkins wrapped in rings made of mother-of-pearl with diamonds. —Leyla Saz, Haremin Icyuzu *(1921)*

Afiyet şeker olsun. (May it turn to sugar.)
Teşekkür ederim, sizede afiyet. (I give you thanks. And yours, too.)

Unknown artist, Harem Scene at Court of Shah Jahan (album leaf), second quarter of 17th century, Ink, colors and gold on paper, 7⅞ x 5 in. (13⅛ x 8¼ in. sheet), The Metropolitan Museum of Art, New York; Theodore M. Davis Collection, Bequest of Theodore M. Davis, 1915

Each meal started with those words before anyone touched a morsel. Eating was not a casual activity in the harem, but an elaborate ritual. All day long, an endless stream of confections and sherbets passed through the corridors to the apartments of the valide sultana, the kadins, and the favorites. Sherbets were by far the most desirable delicacy among the women, most of whom cherished a sweet tooth. Their preparation required a seventy-mile trip from Mount Olympus, where snow from the great ice pits was wrapped in flannel and carried to the Seraglio on mules, according to Evliya Chelebi's travelogue, *Seyahatname* (1314–28). The snow men wore turbans made of snow, and mountains of the purest snow gathered from Mount Olympus, as large as cupolas, were piled on wagons and pulled by a file of seventy to eighty mules. M. de M. D'Ohsson in his eighteenth-century *Tableau général de l'empire ottoman* describes the *Gülhane* (Rose House), where only sherbets and preserves were made: "The care that they took in making sherbets was as intricate as the French took in making their wine. Sherbet would usually be a concoction of different fruit juices, as well as essence of flowers, such as rose, gardenia, pansy, linden flower, and chamomile; and it was perfumed with musk, ambergris, and aloes." Sherbets were made from violets and roses, and coffee flavored with cloves, cinnamon, and rose petals.

Before being served, the sultan's food was tasted for poison in the *Kushane* (Bird House). Impressive stone shelves lined an entire wall in the Food Corridor, where the black eunuchs gathered the brass trays bearing food from the royal kitchens to be distributed in the harem. The food was placed on high marble shelves next to the doors of the sultana's apartments.

Servants carried the trays over their heads and placed them in the center of the room for women to choose as they pleased. Well-trained odalisques waited on the valide sultana, while the kadins and the favorites who had been granted their own apartments ate out of silver trays placed on small low tables. Not until the reign of Mahmud II (1808–39) was silverware introduced to the harem. Before this, the women ate with their hands—maintaining that taste is first transmitted through the fingertips.

Eating with the fingers was a stylized and highly refined art form among the harem women. All odalisques were carefully trained to perform this ritual with delicacy, lightness, and grace. They manipulated the fingers in much the same way as the Japanese do in the tea ceremony, every movement—reaching, bending, turning—becoming a dance of extreme skill and precision. They reserved the right hand for food (the left was for unclean tasks), using only three fingers and scarcely getting the tips soiled.

After a meal, servants delivered a silver pitcher and basin for washing the hands, and towels embroidered with gold and silver for drying them. Then it was time to recline on great cushions and smoke cigarettes or *nargileh* (waterpipes). Tobacco was of very high quality and one of the greatest joys

"A Harem Beauty": fancifully staged impression of a harem inmate by a nineteenth-century American studio. One half of a stereopticon view.

of harem life. Women smoked profusely and indiscriminately—except in the presence of men. The novices, who were not allowed to smoke, did so secretly. Elizabeth Warnock Fernea, in *Guests of the Sheik* (1965), describes the conflict over tobacco between two wives in an Iraqi harem:

> *"It is better not to smoke," said the old woman who had guided me to Selma's door. "Haji Hamid does not like women who smoke."*
>
> *Selma looked at the old woman. "Kulthum," she said, "Haji Hamid is my husband as well as yours," and then deliberately lit cigarettes for herself and several others.*

Chibuks and nargileh added elegance to the smoking ritual. Théophile Gautier himself indulged:

> *Nothing is more propitious to the fostering of poetical reveries than relaxing on the cushions of a divan and inhaling, in short intakes, this fragrant smoke, cooled by the water through which it moves, which reaches the smoker after being propelled through red or green leather tubes that intertwine with his arms, making him somewhat resemble a Cairo snake charmer playing with serpents.*

The gustatory excess that characterized harem life fattened the inmates. "They have . . . crooked feet, and this comes from sitting on the ground cross-wise," Bassano da Zara observed. "For the most part they are fat because they eat a lot of rice with bullock's meat and butter, much more than men do. They do not drink wine, but sugared water, or Cervosa (herb-beer) made in their own manner." By "cervosa" da Zara must have meant *boza,* a fermented barley drink, deliciously sour, served cool, sprinkled with *leblebi* (roasted chick peas) or cinnamon. The best way I know to describe it is something like a brew of sake and tapioca blended together, seasoned with a pinch of sweet vinegar. When I was a child, "boza men," dressed all in white, strolled the streets on autumn nights, bellowing, "Boza, boza, Achman's boza, marvelous bozaaaaa!" They carried on their shoulders brass buckets full of this sweet and sour drink. We would call out their names and run out to the street to have boza poured into our tall glass mugs. When I recently returned to Turkey, these calls of "boza, boza, marvelous boza," the last cry of the Ottoman Empire, no longer echoed through the streets. The drink was about to disappear forever; the only place to get it was an obscure cafe, which called itself "Achman's," in the Ulus district of Ankara. Their boza had neither the charm nor the fine flavor of the drink I recall.

Lunch and dinner were the big meals, always a feast: lamb dishes, *börek*

Paul-Desiré
Trouillebert,
The Harem
Servant, 1874,
Oil on canvas,
51⅛ x 38⅛ in.,
Musée des Beaux-
Arts, Nice

(pastries filled with meat, cheese, or spinach), pilav, eggplant, choices of vegetables specially cooked in olive oil, and always lots of rich desserts and compotes. And then a mid-evening snack of fruits and cakes.

Many of the harem women were highly evolved confectioners and frequently gave an assortment of sweets as gifts to one another. Among these, Turkish delight was the most desired. Several thousand tons were—and still are—exported annually. This chewy paste is made from the pulp of white grapes or mulberries, semolina flour, honey, rose water, and assorted nuts, rejoicing in the name *Rahat Lokum*—"to give rest to the throat," a rest absolutely essential after a harem feast.

Other pastries and desserts had voluptuous and erotic names like "Lips of the Beauty," "Hanum's Fingers," "Ladies' Thighs," or "Woman's Navel."

Lips of the Beauty

Syrup:	*Rolls:*
2½ cups sugar	½ stick butter
1 tsp lemon juice	1¾ cups water
3 cups water	1½ cups flour
	1 tsp salt
	2 beaten eggs & 1 egg yolk
	1 cup safflower oil

Make a syrup, mixing together the sugar, lemon juice, and water; boil for 15 minutes, stirring occasionally. Set aside to cool.

Heat butter in a saucepan until it begins to change color. Add the flour and the salt to make a paste and slowly pour in the water. Cook over very low heat for about 10 minutes, stirring constantly. Remove from heat and cool to room temperature. Add the two eggs and the yolk slowly, and beat well with a fork until blended. Turn on a floured board and knead thoroughly. Divide the dough into walnut-size pieces and shape into rolls folded over like Parker House rolls, to resemble lips. Heat the oil and place the lip-shaped rolls in it. Fry on both sides until golden brown. Remove and drain off excess oil. Pour the syrup over it and serve warm.

This is a sickeningly sweet dessert we loved as children. Great-aunt Meryem was the confectioner in our family, and she kept us very happy with Lips of Beauty and her yogurt dessert.

After these totally satisfying and exhausting sweets came the great coffee ritual. One attendant brought in the coffee, another carried a tray with diamond-studded accoutrements, a third actually served the coffee. Turkish coffee was not grown in Turkey but came from Yemen—and initially met a hostile reception. It was considered a source of immorality and was banned for many years. By the mid seventeenth century, its virtues were extolled with deliberate Turkish extravagance in such works as Katib Chelebi's *The Balance of Truth* (1650), which claimed, among other things, that boiling-hot coffee miraculously causes no burns:

> *Coffee is indubitably cold and dry. Even when it is boiled in water and an infusion made of it, its coldness does not depart: perhaps it increases, for water too is cold. That is why coffee quenches thirst, and does not burn if poured on a limb, for its heat is a strange heat, with no effect.*
>
> *To those of moist temperament, and especially to women, it is highly suited. They should drink a great deal of strong coffee. Excess of it will do them no harm, so long as they are not melancholic.*

What distinguishes Turkish coffee is its texture of very finely ground grains, almost pulverized, and its idiosyncratic method of preparation.

Turkish Coffee

½ cup water	2 tsp pulverized coffee
2 Tbsp sugar	

Pour cold water in a jezve (a small cylindrical pot with a long handle). Add sugar and coffee. Stir well. Place over low flame and heat until small bubbles barely begin to form. Remove from the flame and pour off froth into demitasse cups. Bring to boil, but do not allow it to boil over. Remove from flame. Pour coffee over the froth to fill cups and serve.

It seems like a very simple operation, but making it perfectly is one of the most difficult things in the world. It has to have just the right amount of froth, and this is a function of timing.

Coffee making was a crucially important part of a young woman's life, since her merits as a wife were initially and continually evaluated on the basis of how her coffee tasted. She painstakingly practiced to get it just right, in order to win the heart of her beloved's mother.

I myself went through an intensive training when I was about nine years old and assumed somehow that this custom of one generation of women teaching a younger generation would survive forever. But this, too, is a vanishing tradition. Indeed, Turkish coffee was nearly obsolete when I recently returned. Everyone now favored "Néscafe," which meant *any* kind of instant coffee; to ask for Turkish coffee was old-fashioned and gauche.

Above:
Isma'il Jala'ir,
Ladies round a
samovar, *third
quarter of the
19th century,
Oil on canvas,
Victoria and Albert
Museum, London*

*Turkish harem
women without their
veils*

It was not considered good form for women in harems to drink alcohol, but they did serve the men *raki,* a beverage made from distilled grapes and flavored with anise, similar to Greek ouzo or French absinthe. This colorless liquid turns milky white like eau de cologne when ice or water is added to it. No mild libation, it is called "Lion's Milk."

In contrast to the other meals, breakfast in harems was simple and modest, consisting of clotted cream, honey, feta cheese, jams, and olives, with strong Russian tea—never coffee. In fact, it is still considered inappropriate to order coffee for breakfast. Simple—but, in the case of the royal

Camille Rogier, Women in the Imperial Harem, *Oil, Topkapi Museum, Istanbul*

Me at nine years old, learning to dance, sing, and brew good Turkish coffee

harem, still special, as Leyla Saz recalled in *Haremin İçyüzü*: "Certain cream cheeses and feta cheeses were made in silver containers and delivered to the palace in baskets. These special treats were for the Royal Palace only and were never sold elsewhere. In return for these delicacies, the merchant would be rewarded with stuffed mussels."

Cleopatra is reputed to have had twenty-four kitchens, one for every hour. In the Seraglio there were ten double (or twenty single) kitchens allocated to the sultan, the valide sultana, the kadins, the eunuchs, and other members of the court. That was impressive enough to Ottaviano Bon (*Narrative of Travels,* 1604):

> *The kitchen utensils are a sight to see, because the pots, cauldrons, and other necessary things are so huge and nearly all of copper that of things of this kind it would be impossible to see any more beautiful or better kept. The service of dishes is of copper tinned over, and kept in such continual good repair and so spotless that it is an amazing sight to behold. There is an enormous quantity of them, and they are a very considerable expense to the Porte, and especially because the kitchens provide food for so many both within and without, particularly on the four days of the Public Divan (a time when an extra 4,000 to 5,000 would be fed, in addition to the usual 1,000 or more). . . .*

The royal kitchens had 150 cooks, the most prestigious position among them being the dresser of the sultan's food. According to Nicolas de Nicolay, who visited the Seraglio in 1551, "Those of the privy kitchens have their furnaces apart, to dress and make ready the meat without the smell of smoke, which, being sodden and dressed, they lay in platters of porcelain, and so deliver it unto the Cecigners, whom we do call carvers, to serve the same unto the great lord, the taste [for poison] being made in his presence."

The wood to keep the braziers burning and to stoke the fires in the harem kitchens came from the sultan's own forests. Thirty enormous lumberjacks in the service of the Seraglio sailed the Black Sea regularly to keep the stockpiles high, taking slaves along with them to cut and load the wood.

When I asked my grandmother what food it was the women of the harem really loved the best, I expected to hear something like a very exotic form of baklava. "Eggplant, of course," she said. "It's the most enchanted food. We believed in those days that if a woman dreamed of eggplant, she would be pregnant. We drank its bitter juice to flush down the ifrits. We scrubbed our faces with it. But mostly we had to know a thousand ways to cook it in order to win a man's heart. You have to know at least fifty," she told me. "Otherwise, you will be an old maid."

*Jean-Joseph
Benjamin-Constant,
Harem, ca. 1885,
Oil on canvas,
40 x 30 in.,
Private collection*

Sultanas

Live among diamonds and splendor as the wife of the sultan!
　　　　　　　　　　　　　　—Circassian lullaby

Marriage of Sultans

In 1346, the marriage between Sultan Orhan and the Byzantine princess Theodora was celebrated with incredible pomp and ceremony on the European shores of Constantinople, which did not yet belong to the Ottomans. Orhan, camped on the Asian shore, sent a fleet of thirty vessels and an escort of cavalry to retrieve his purple bride. "At a signal," Edward Gibbon wrote in *The Decline and Fall of the Roman Empire,* "the curtains were suddenly drawn, to disclose the bride, or the victim, encircled by kneeling eunuchs and hymeneal torches; the sound of flutes and trumpets proclaimed the joyful event; and her pretended happiness was the theme of the nuptial song, which was chanted by such poets as the age could produce. Without the rites of the church, Theodora was delivered to her barbarous lord; but it had been stipulated that she could preserve her religion in the harem of Bursa."

In the early years of the Ottoman Empire, the sultans married daughters of Byzantine emperors, Anatolian princes, and Balkan kings. These marriages were strictly diplomatic arrangements. After the conquest of Constantinople, the royal harem became populated with non-Turkish odalisques. This tradition continued until the fall of the empire. Since these slave girls were his property, in accordance with Islamic law, the sultan was not required to marry any of them. But, once in a while, a sultan—such as Süleyman the Magnificent—chose to marry a special woman.

In contrast to the odalisques, a sultan's concubines were considered his wives, *kadinlar* or *kadinefendiler,* the number varying from four to eight. The first wife was called *bash kadin* (head woman), followed by *ikinci kadin* (second), *uchuncu* (third), and on down. If any one of the kadins died, the others below her moved up a rank, but not before the chief black eunuch delivered the sultan's approval for such a promotion.

It is a common fantasy to imagine sultans actually having sexual relations with hundreds of women in their harem. In some cases, this might have been true. For example, when Murad III died, over a hundred cradles were being rocked. But several sultans chose to take only one kadin—Selim

I, Mehmed III, Murad IV, Ahmed II—and as far as we can conjecture, they remained faithful to these women.

Most sultans spent nights with different of their favored women in turn, and to prevent disputes among them, they kept a schedule. The *haznedar* (the chief treasurer) recorded each "couching" in a special diary in

Jean-Léon Gérôme, Palace Guard, 1865, Oil on panel, 13½ x 9½ in., The Fine Art Society, London. The guard depicted here is a halberdier keeping evening watch.

order to establish the birth and legitimacy of the children. This extraordinary chronicle, which survives today, discloses not only sexual intimacies but also such historical events as the execution of Gülfem Kadin, one of Süleyman's wives, for selling her "couching" turn to another woman. Much to the chagrin of Western minds, there seem to have been no outright orgies involving the sultan and his many women. It is not difficult to assume, however, that some of the more debauched and insane rulers, like Ibrahim, did indulge in less routine sexual rituals.

A sultan's failure to favor each wife with equal enthusiasm stirred up a great deal of anxiety, insecurity—and malevolence. Mahidevran Sultana, for example, mutilated Roxalena's face, Gülnush Sultana pushed the odalisque Gülbeyaz off a cliff, Hürrem Sultana was strangled, Bezmialem Sultana mysteriously vanished. Each glass of sherbet potentially contained poison. There were alliances, cliques, and a perpetual silent war. This ambience affected not only the emotional climate of the harem but also state politics. "The rigorous discipline, which turns the harem into a prison, is justified by the passionate disposition of these women, which may impel them to who knows what aberrations," commented historian Alain Grosrichard in *Structure du serail* (1979).

If an odalisque became sexually involved with a prince, she was likely to become his wife when he ascended the throne. Wives could not sit in the presence of the sultan without permission, and on all occasions they were highly mannered, talking and acting with great ceremony. The mothers of the princes always received their sons standing up and addressed them as "My Lion." The relationships among the wives were formal. When they wished to talk with one another, the *kalfa* (secretary) officially conveyed the request. Harem etiquette required treating elders with respect and courtesy. All the women were expected to kiss the skirts of the wives out of traditional respect; often, out of courtesy, the wives asked them not to. Princes always kissed the hands of their father's kadins.

Harem Women and Politics

The excessive interference of the harem women in state politics was instrumental in the decline and fall of the empire. Ironically, such meddling began during the reign of Suleyman the Magnificent, the most powerful period in the empire's history (1520–66). It was then that the women moved with Roxalena from the Old Palace, built by Mehmed the Conqueror, to the Seraglio harem (1541), and approached the seat of power. This marked the beginning of the Sultanate, or the Reign of Women, which lasted a century and a half, until the end of the struggle between Kösem and Turhan sultanas (1687).

After Suleyman's death, the sultans no longer led their armies in campaign or in battle, retiring instead to the womb of the harem. They detached themselves from world affairs and spent most of their time in the company of women. This royal seclusion greatly diminished their ability to govern, and in varying degrees, sultanas began wielding influence over state officials, with bribery and patronage supplanting promotion on the basis of merit. A succession of child sultans and mentally deranged ones after Mehmed III's death in 1603 made women the power behind the throne.

It is fascinating to note how these ladies turned their disadvantaged situation to advantage. Every empire has experienced the behind-the-scenes influence of certain legendary women, such as Madame Pompadour or China's Dowager Empress Jung-shu, but in no other nation's history do we actually see them in command—albeit secretly—of so much power. From their luxurious prison, they bent the court, the *Divan* (Chancery of State), and the entire Seraglio to their will. Through the chief eunuchs, they communicated to the grand vizier and other important political figures and sometimes even held interviews through a curtain or a latticed window. They gained knowledge not only of the court but also of the rest of the world, at times overthrowing their enemies and elevating allies. They elected governors and even formed intrigues with foreign countries.

For example, the Venetian Baffa, who became Sultana Safiye, had been captured by Turkish corsairs en route to Corfu, where her father, of the noble Baffo family, was the governor. Sold to the harem of Murad IV, she was determined to look after the interests of Venice, as a form of vengeance. Even when Venetian naval vessels offered insult and injury to Turkish shipping, she was able to dissuade the sultan from attacking her native Saint Mark's, and to persuade him to give Venice especially favorable commercial advantages.

Both the Venetian ambassador and Catherine de Medici communicated with Baffa through a Jewess, Chiarezza (Kira), who posed as a bundle woman, bringing cloth and jewels to the Seraglio. Seduced by the gifts sent to her by Queen Elizabeth I, Baffa pledged assistance to the English, both in state and trade affairs. She personally corresponded with the queen—treason, under Ottoman law. Her son, Sultan Mehmed III, was aware of Baffa's dubious activities but revered her too much to interfere. Nevertheless, Baffa ended her days miserably, mysteriously strangled in her bed in 1583. A

*Melchior Lorchs,
Süleyman the
Magnificent, 1559,
Engraving,
12⅜ x 17⅛ in.,
The British Museum,
London.
Süleyman the
Magnificent was the
first sultan ever to
marry a woman in his
harem—Roxalena.*

Genoese paper reported the death of this woman who had been born in the rival city-state of Venice: "La stata assasine aquella Sultana, che si chiama La Sporca, che le fu una vecchia materola." (That wicked old woman, the filthy Sultana, has been assassinated.)

Valide Procession

A shift of power began with the ascension of each new sultan. A new woman became valide. In a splendid procession, sometimes involving as many as a hundred beautiful carriages, along a road lined with *Janissaries* (soldiers), she was transported by litter from the House of Tears to the Seraglio. Her steward trailed behind, bearing a scepter and the heralds of the Divan, accompanied by another high palace official who scattered coins to the people watching the procession. Coaches carrying the odalisques and other members of the sultan's retinue followed. At the Imperial Gate, the sultan, riding on a horse, met his mother, kissed her hand, and led her into the harem of the Seraglio.

Princess Sultanas

The sultan's daughters grew up playing with other royal children and the child odalisques in the Seraglio. Like their brothers, they were formally educated at the palace school until they reached puberty.

Pierre Auguste Renoir, A Girl with a Falcon (Mlle. Fleury in Algerian costume), 1880, Oil on canvas, 49¹³/₁₆ x 30¼ in., Sterling and Francine Clark Art Institute, Williamstown, Massachusetts

Marriages of the princesses were mostly political arrangements, as in most other monarchies. The sultan chose the husbands for his daughters and sisters, and the grand vizier served the decree formally. As soon as a prospective groom received such a decree, he was required to divorce his former wives and odalisques.

Until the early nineteenth century, the princesses were married to important statesmen much older than themselves. Consequently, they often became widows at an early age. Some of the girls were only two or three years old when they were betrothed. In the annals of the Seraglio, there is a beautiful recollection of the wedding (1709) between the five-year-old Princess Fatma, daughter of Ahmed III, and his courtier, Ali Pasha, who was a middle-aged man. The ceremony was symbolic, and the bridegroom was required to wait for eight years before beginning the marriage in fact, never being permitted unchaperoned in his wife's presence until the princess reached puberty. However, this marriage was never consummated, because Ali Pasha was killed in battle seven years after the ceremony, before the princess came of age.

During the nineteenth century, the practice of child marriage was ended and puberty declared the minimum age for marriage. Some of the princesses were even allowed to select their own husbands, thereby achieving greater freedom than any other women in Islamic society. Some actually married for love; some married several times.

The sultans spent lavishly on their daughters' weddings, and the bride's trousseau was displayed to the public, as Baron Helmuth von Moltke reported in 1836, on the occasion of Mihrimah Sultana's wedding:

> *Yesterday (Wednesday, May 4, 1836) the princess's trousseau was taken to her new residence. Guarded by cavalrymen and preceded by several pashas, the procession consisted of forty mules loaded with bales of precious cloth, twenty coaches loaded with shawls, carpets, silk garments and other items, and behind these, three hundred and sixty porters bearing large silver trays on their heads. On first of these trays was a splendid Koran with a gold binding set with pearls, followed by silver chairs, braziers, boxes of jewellry, gold bird cages and the Lord knows what else. Probably some of these things would be secretly returned to the treasury to be displayed again at the next marriage of a princess.*

Feasting, dancing, music, fireworks often lasted for several weeks. Every day of the wedding, a new form of entertainment was organized. People in all parts of the city were entertained by drummers, jugglers, acrobats, wrestlers, and cockfights. After the ceremony and feasting, the newlyweds moved to a palace that the sultan had bought and furnished for them. The bridegroom entered the bride's chamber, accompanied by the chief black eunuch. He performed his prayers first, then crawled to the bed and kissed the princess's feet. Thus began the nuptial night.

Some of the princesses, like Süleyman the Magnificent's daughter Mihrimah and his granddaughter Ayshe Humashah, wielded a great deal of power over their fathers and husbands. Hatice Sultana, another daughter of Ahmed III (1703–30), was the real power during the Tulip Era, influencing the sultan and her husband, the grand vizier, while indulging in intrigues with the Marquis de Villeneuve, furthering the cause of France in its war with Russia.

Remarriage of Sultanas

The sultans frequently offered in marriage to other men of power those wives who were unable to conceive or those who had produced a stillbirth. Marriages were also arranged for odalisques and childless favorites.

When a sultan died, his favorites were no longer *the* favorites. Suddenly deprived of all privileges, they were sent to the House of Tears, and a new harem was established in the Seraglio. Sometimes the widows remarried.

Accouchement and Birth

In preparation for birth, one of the larger kiosks in the Seraglio was cleaned impeccably and decorated. The bedcovers and the quilts were red. The washing bowls, ewers, and other utensils, either gold or silver.

Sitting, rather than lying down, was considered the most natural position for delivery, and special birthing chairs were used. An entourage of ladies-in-waiting kept the mother company while the midwife delivered the baby. The wet-nurse took over immediately after birth. Sometimes singers, dancers, or the palace dwarf, who was a eunuch, were invited in to distract the woman during labor. The entire event was treated more like a celebration than an ordeal.

As soon as the child was born, the chief black eunuch spread the news to the rest of the palace. Each department sacrificed five rams for a boy child and three rams for a girl. The cannons fired seven rounds for a boy and three for a girl, repeating fives times during twenty-four hours, once for each call to prayer. The valide sultana and the grand vizier arranged audiences, presenting the baby, the mother, and the other women of power in

Birth chair, early 18th century

Right:
Husein Fazil Enderuni,
An Accouchement
in the Harem,
Miniature from
Zanan-Name,
17th century,
Istanbul University
Library. A sultana in
labor sits on a special
birth chair while she
is entertained by her
odalisques and the
palace dwarf, a
eunuch.

the harem with fine gifts. Exquisite cradles, inlaid with gems, and jeweled quilts awaited the arrival of the royal babies. Town criers spread the news to the inhabitants of the city; poets immortalized the happy event in verse and song.

The harem was transformed into a world of light and color, bustling with a great deal of activity during the week-long birth celebrations. Lanterns, lamps, and torches illuminated the interior and the exterior. Wealthy Ottoman gentry showed off their wares in extravagance. During that one week, the entire city turned into a spectacle out of *One Thousand and One Nights*.

Death of Sultanas

A great deal of mystery surrounds the woman who sleeps next to Mehmed the Conqueror in a nameless coffin. The *mullahs* (Moslem theologians) claim it is Irene, later declared an Orthodox saint, with whom the sultan had become obsessed: "He not only consumed dayes and nights with her but burned with continual jealousie," according to William Pointer's 1566 allegory *Palace of Pleasure*.

He offered her everything, but Irene would not abjure her faith. The mullahs reproached the sultan for courting a *gavur* (infidel). According to Richard Davey's *Sultan and His Subjects* (1897), one day Mehmed gathered all the mullahs in the courtyard of his palace. Irene stood in the center, concealed under a glittering veil, which the Sultan slowly lifted, revealing her exquisite beauty. "You see, she is more beautiful than any woman you have ever seen," he said, "lovelier than the houries of your dreams. And I love her more than I do my own life. But my life is worthless compared to my love for Islam." He seized and twisted the long, golden tresses of Irene and, with one stroke of his scimitar, severed her head from her body. In his poem *Irene* (1708), Charles Goring immortalizes this excruciating moment:

> *Jealous of Empire and my lost Renown,*
> *I stabb'd a Mistress, to preserve my Crown,*
> *But had the faire returned my generous flames,*
> *I'd slighted Empire and embraced the Dame.*

Süleyman the Magnificent ordered the execution of his kadin Gülfem when she failed one night to appear in his bed. During one of his debauches, the mad Sultan Ibrahim ordered all his women seized during the night, stuffed in sacks, and thrown into the Bosphorus. One was saved by French sailors and taken to Paris, where she must have had some stories to tell.

Among the many powerful and interesting sultanas who lived, loved, and ruled in the Seraglio, three deserve special attention. Each embodies the nuances of the century in which she lived. Roxalena (1526–58) was the first woman legally to marry a sultan, move into the Seraglio with her entourage, and gain complete ascendancy over the greatest of the sultans, Süleyman the Magnificent. Kösem Sultana reigned the longest and saw the most. And Nakshedil Sultana—Aimée de Rivery—lived the sort of life legends are made of.

Roxalena (Hürrem Sultana)

On the third of Istanbul's seven hills rises the Mosque of Süleyman the Magnificent, the most glorious silhouette above the promontory. It is colossal and imposing, but it also has a capricious charm, reflecting the genius and exuberant spirit of its architect, Sinan. Numerous smaller domes are scattered whimsically around the central dome, like soap bubbles. Four stiletto minarets soar above the skyline.

Inside, the mosque is dark and somber, despite the beautiful windows of jeweled Persian glass and colorful tiles around the *mihrab* (niche indicating Mecca). Its quiet dimness, its silence and desertion make it seem peaceful, almost ethereal, as is the garden in back, which shelters the mausoleums of Süleyman and his legendary wife Roxalena. A grapevine straggles over the

Portrait of Roxalena (Hürrem Sultana), 16th century, Topkapi Palace Portrait Gallery, Istanbul

walls of their tombs, and a profusion of blood-red amaranthus, the flower known as "love lies bleeding," sprouts out of the earth.

The lovers slumber in their graves, once the most powerful mortals of this city, now sacks of bones. It makes one think of Istanbul's contradictions: the Bosphorus separating two continents, unable to make up its mind where its allegiance lies, caught between wealth and starvation, between the physical and the spiritual, the sacred and profane. The prayer chant from the minaret wafts like smoke over the rooftops of the city, just as it must have done when Roxalena was alive.

As with most of the women who passed through the harems, Roxalena's origins are shrouded in mystery. Presumably she was a Russian slave from the Ukraine—which might explain the name "Roxalena" or "Russalena"—purchased at the open-air market by Süleyman's best friend, the grand vizier, Ibrahim (no relation to the mad sultan of that name).

Her portraits suggest a mosaic refinement, with classical features and blazing red hair. There is depth and intelligence in her eyes. An extraordinary strategist and a true political artist, Roxalena planned her moves as if she were playing chess.

At the beginning, Süleyman was attracted to her silent charm, and she became his favorite. Soon she bore him a son, which elevated her to third kadin—the third most powerful woman in the hierarchy of the harem. Roxalena was aware that, according to the Code of Laws established by Mehmed the Conqueror, the throne passed to the oldest male, obliging him to get rid of all his brothers in order to secure it for his own offspring. As such, from the beginning, Prince Mustafa, the heir apparent, was the death warrant of her own male children.

In 1526, Pietro Bragadino, Venetian *bailie* (ambassador) in Istanbul, reported to the Venetian Senate a vicious quarrel between the two sultanas, in which Gülbahar Sultana, first kadin and Mustafa's mother, pulled Roxalena's hair and scratched her face badly. Roxalena confined herself in her apartments, refusing to appear before Süleyman, using her disfigurement as an excuse. She continued withholding her favors, demanding that Süleyman marry her legally and consent to share not only pleasure but power. This obstinacy might well have cost Roxalena her life, but Süleyman was impressed by her sharp mind and her fearlessness. To please her, he sent his son Prince Mustafa to be a governor of Manisa, far from the seat of power. Mustafa's mother, Gülbahar, accompanied him, in accordance with protocol. To cement his fidelity to Roxalena, Süleyman slowly released his other concubines, marrying off many of the most beautiful women to his pashas.

He acceded to her every wish, including marriage, and Roxalena became the first woman to marry a sultan officially—the significance of which did not escape a contemporary English observer, Sir George Young (1530):

> This week there has occurred in this city a most extraordinary event, one absolutely unprecedented in the history of the sultans. The Grand Signor Suleiman has taken to himself as his Empress a slave woman from Russia, called Roxalena, and there has been great feasting. The ceremony took place in the Seraglio, and the festivities have been beyond all record. There was a public procession of the presents. At night the principal streets were gaily illuminated and there is much music and feasting. The Houses are festooned with garlands and there are everywhere swings in which the people swing by the hour with great enjoyment. In the old Hippodrome a great tribune is set up, the place reserved for the Empress and her ladies screened with gilt lattice. Here Roxalena and the court attended a great tournament in which both Christian and Moslem Knights were engaged, and tumblers and jugglers and a procession of wild beasts, and giraffes with necks so long they, as it were, touched the sky. . . . There is a great deal of talk about the marriage and none can say what it means.

And Süleyman became distinguished as the first sultan to submit to the paramount influence of a woman. "The only unfavorable thing one could cite against Süleyman is his excessive devotion to his wife," wrote the Hapsburg envoy. This beautiful, ambitious woman ruled over Süleyman until her death thirty-two years later. Da Zara reflected:

> He bears her such love and keeps such faith to her that all of his subjects marvel and say that she has bewitched him, and they call her the ziadi [jadi], or the witch. On this account the army and the court hate her and her children, but because he loves her, no one dares to protest: For myself I have always heard every one speak ill of her and of her children, and well of the first-born and his mother.

Süleyman was a poet. He loved the language of poetry, and within Roxalena was the blood of a poet as well. They courted each other through verse, her voice carrying through the fields of battle, muting the sounds of cannon and slashing swords. Süleyman had found a woman who was his match, who not only fulfilled him in bed but also became his companion in affairs of state and in a shared appreciation of the arts. The harem was transformed into a place of beauty, a place of enlightenment, rather than a dark dungeon.

Roxalena was so full of light that Süleyman seemed blind to her dark side. He named her Hürrem, "the laughing one," because of her crystalline laughter and freedom from inhibition.

Yet Hürrem was secretly tormented. In 1541, when the Old Palace, which housed the sultan's harem, partially burned down, Roxalena, with her entourage of odalisques and eunuchs, moved to the Grand Seraglio, where she could be closer to Süleyman and the seat of power, a move that marked the beginning of the Grand Harem and "The Reign of Women."

With Mustafa and Gülbahar tucked far away, Roxalena had still another antagonist to deal with, the man who had originally owned her, the inseparable friend and companion of Süleyman, Ibrahim, who shared Süleyman's tent and his dreams, who had been promoted from the status of royal falconer to Lord of Rumelia and, later, grand vizier. Ibrahim had been chosen to marry the sultan's own sister, Hatice Sultana, and had been the object of endless wealth and honor. He may have presented Roxalena to Süleyman as a move to consolidate his power; if so, the scheme backfired.

Anton Ignaz Melling, Interior of the Palace of Hatice Sultana, *Etching reproduced in* Views of Constantinople and the Bosphorous, *ca. 1815*

Grown resentful of his influence and jealous of Süleyman's affection for him, Roxalena set out to orchestrate his death. She took advantage of every bit of gossip and information to inflame Süleyman's mind against his friend. One night, when Ibrahim was in the Seraglio as a privileged friend of the sultan, the deaf-mute guards strangled him in his sleep. Roxalena may have been responsible for Ibrahim's assassination, and there are many who have accused her of it, but there is no conclusive evidence.

Some time after this, Süleyman declared to Roxalena that he wanted to build her a new palace. She feared that putting her out of sight might mean putting her out of mind—and, eventually, out of favor. To distract Süleyman, she came up with a more challenging project: a mosque to be built by the greatest architect of the time, Sinan, and to be named after the sultan himself, the Süleymaniye, the Mosque of Süleyman the Magnificent. Once again she triumphed. The year was 1549.

As Roxalena's sons grew older, Prince Mustafa loomed as a greater and greater obstacle. He was an able and intelligent prince, much admired by the people and the army. He was also Süleyman's favorite son. How to cause his fall from grace?

A forged letter supposedly written by Mustafa to the shah of Persia, declaring that he wanted to dethrone his father and asking for the shah's assistance, turned father against son and provoked battle on the plains of Ereğli. It is said that several times both Süleyman and Mustafa turned back as they rode to the field, but fate urged them forward: history had already been written by kismet.

Mustafa ran to his father, alone, unarmed, to redeem himself. He reached the sultan's tent, going through four partitions. When he came to the fifth, his cries echoed through the plains. It is said that Süleyman shed tears for the son he had killed, and for the father who could kill such a son.

Of Roxalena's four sons, Mehmed died young of natural causes; Cihangir, possessed of a brilliant mind, was deformed and epileptic; Beyazit was able but cruel. Selim was her choice as heir, because she was convinced that his soft nature would not allow him to murder his brothers. She also knew that Selim drank to dull his prophetic awareness of impending death. Risking Süleyman's wrath, she was not reluctant to supply the wine to ease her son's pain. He became known as Selim the Sot.

But no matter how much Roxalena plotted, she could not alter kismet. She did not live to realize her dream of becoming the valide sultana. Nor did she live to see the twist of fate that set brother against brother, father against son. She would not see the struggle for the throne between Selim and Beyazit, which drove Beyazit to take refuge with the shah of Persia. She would not see how Süleyman forced the shah to extradite Beyazit, and how he promptly assassinated him, as well as the shah and his sons.

Roxalena died in 1558. Her place was occupied by her daughter Mihrimah and her granddaughter Aysha Humashah. Selim the Sot and his son Murad III both preferred women and pleasure to political matters. Their sisters, wives, and daughters took full advantage of the weak nature of the pair, dabbling in politics and securing important posts for their own husbands and sons. It was Mihrimah, rather than his sons, that Süleyman consulted on important issues.

Roxalena had trained her daughter well.

Kösem

Princes Ahmed and Mustafa lived together in the Golden Cage. When Ahmed became sultan, he did not have the heart to murder his brother, but he did keep Mustafa in the Cage—with just a few women. He built a wall to block the entrance, leaving a small window through which food was passed to Mustafa, as well as alcohol and opium. Fourteen years later, this same wall was hammered down, and the utterly demented Mustafa was declared sultan.

His own years of isolation had created in Ahmed a void that consumed continual diversion. He took a different woman to bed each night, but he favored the Greek beauty Kösem, lavishing on her the finest jewels from his hoard. Kösem was fifteen years old when she became the favorite of fifteen-year-old Ahmed I.

Ahmed ruled from 1603 to 1617, leaving Kösem a young widow. Mustafa was released from the Cage, to become sultan, while Kösem's own sons, Murad, Beyazit, and Ibrahim, took his place there. After only a few months, the crazed Mustafa was dethroned by the eunuch corps, who did not favor him, and returned to the Cage. Mustafa's son Osman succeeded him, but the young sultan fell victim to the uprising of the janissaries and the *sipahis* (cavalry). Troops marched into the Seraglio and dragged the sultan to the common Yedikule (Seven Towers) prison. He was murdered, his ear cut off and presented to his mother as an affront. Although fratricide was common in the Ottoman Empire, this was the first act of regicide. Once again, mad Mustafa was dragged out of the Cage (1622) and enthroned. This time he ordered the execution of Kösem's sons. The eunuch corps—again—intervened and crowned Kösem's oldest son as Murad IV (1623–40).

Thus Kösem attained her ambition of becoming valide sultana. But Murad's cruelty disturbed her. He passed a law prohibiting drinking and smoking throughout the empire, while he himself abused both habits. He ordered the execution of anyone else breaking this law. In a drunken stupor and accompanied by a mysterious dervish, Murad wandered the streets incognito, searching for victims. Corpses hung at every street corner.

Kösem's youngest son, Ibrahim, was also deranged. She set her hopes on handsome, astute, and brave Beyazit, who was highly skilled in jousting. One day, Beyazit threw Murad off in a joust. Shortly thereafter, while campaigning in Persia, Beyazit was killed by order of his brother, an incident that later inspired Racine's tragedy *Bejazit*.

It was debauchery that brought about Murad's demise. On his death-bed, he told his mother how much he disdained his brother Ibrahim, and how it would be better for the dynasty to end rather than continue with insane royal seed. He ordered Ibrahim's death, but Kösem intervened, and Ibrahim was ordered out of the Cage. He was too terrified to come out, convinced that his cruel brother was playing a trick to torment him. He refused to leave until Murad's corpse had been brought before him, and even then Kösem had to coax him out as if cajoling a frightened kitten with food.

It was Ibrahim's reign (1640–48) that marked Kösem's real power as valide. With the help of the grand vizier, Mustafa Pasha, the empire was

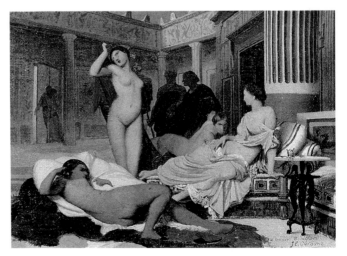

Jean-Léon Gérôme,
Greek Interior,
1848, Oil on canvas,
Musée d'Orsay, Paris

hers to rule. Feeble Ibrahim, entirely absorbed in the joys of the harem, was being devoured by lust and debauchery. The French called him "Le Fou de Fourrures" because of his obsession with furs; he wanted to touch, feel, and see furs everywhere in the harem. He searched the empire for its fattest woman. She was an Armenian, with whom he became madly infatuated, declaring her the Governor General of Damascus. Favored ladies were allowed to take what they pleased from the bazaars. He made his sisters serve the odalisques and presented his odalisques with the wealthiest imperial estates. In a night of madness, he had his entire harem put in sacks and drowned.

It would have been better for the empire if Ibrahim had remained childless. But Kösem was determined to hold power as long as possible. She employed a man named Cinci Hoca (Keeper of the Djinns) to concoct various herbs of fertility. Perhaps they were all too effective; Ibrahim had six sons, one after another.

Tales of Ibrahim's madness spread over the empire, finally provoking the janissaries to mutiny; they marched to the Gates of Felicity and demanded the sultan's head. Kösem pleaded with them for several hours. She surrendered when they promised not to kill him but instead to put him back in the Cage. Confined once again, Ibrahim became a raving lunatic. His cries pierced through the thick walls day and night. Ten days after his incarceration, he was strangled by order of the *Mufti* (the head *imam, or* Moslem priest).

Ibrahim's seven-year-old son, Mehmed, by Turhan Sultana, became the new sultan. Kösem had no intention of relinquishing the office of valide to Turhan, and she refused to move to the House of Tears. She schemed to have Mehmed poisoned, so that she could elevate to the throne a young orphan prince whom she could manipulate. A war of two sultanas began. The year was 1651.

The janissaries supported Kösem, but the new grand vizier, Köprülü Mehmed Pasha, and the rest of the palace administration favored Turhan. Kösem conspired to admit the janissaries into the harem one night to dispatch the young sultan and his mother. But Turhan had been informed about this conspiracy. Kösem found herself facing the eunuch corps instead, supporters of Turhan, who demanded her life.

She went mad, stuffing her precious jewels into her pockets and fleeing through the intricate mazes of the harem, which she knew better than anyone. She crept into a small cabinet, hoping that the eunuchs would go past her and the janissaries come to the rescue. But a piece of her skirt caught in

Leon Bakst,
Yellow Sultana,
ca. 1912, Crayon,
watercolor, gouache,
and gold and silver
paint on paper,
18½ x 27 in.,
Private collection

the door, betraying her hiding place. The eunuchs dragged her out, tearing her clothes, stealing her jewels. She fought; but she was an old woman now. One of her attackers strangled her with a curtain. Her naked, bleeding body was dragged outside and flaunted before the janissaries.

Kösem had enjoyed the longest reign of any of the harem women, almost half a century. But she died in horror and abject loneliness.

Turhan triumphed. Her son a child, she assumed absolute power. While she was well liked in the harem, Turhan was a simple woman, unsophisticated in state affairs. With her death in 1687, the Reign of Women came to an end.

Aimée Debucq de Rivery (Nakshedil Sultana)

No sultana is more intriguing than Nakshedil. Her life is shrouded in such mystery that, to this day, no one is sure whether Nakshedil and Aimée de Rivery, the fair, blue-eyed girl from Martinique, were indeed one and the same. I learned about her from an early age because she figured in my own family history—or so said my grandmother Zehra. Among Zehra's many stories was the one about my great-great-grandmother Naime. It went like this.

During the reign of Sultan Abdulaziz, some time in the middle of the last century, the French Empress Eugénie came to Istanbul. The empress wanted to visit the women in the sultan's harem; this was arranged, and the ladies met. They fascinated one another, but could not converse.

"Is there any among you who speaks French?" the empress managed to convey. They all looked at each other, whispered, and shook their heads.

"Then," my grandmother continued, "an old woman spoke up: 'Before Nakshedil Sultana died, there was a young girl she liked. She named her Naime because it sounded,' she said, 'like her own name before she was brought. She taught this girl, herself, the language of the French. And I think the girl still lives in the Old Palace.'"

Immediately Naime was delivered from the darkness of the Palace of the Unwanted Ones and brought to the empress. She was a shy little girl, but she indeed spoke fluent French, with a Martinique accent.

When the sultan saw how much Empress Eugénie liked this forgotten girl, he offered Naime to her as a present to take back with her to France. However, a young man in Eugénie's entourage fell in love with Naime and finally asked the empress for Naime's hand in marriage. At this, the sultan intervened, saying the girl was a Moslem and the only way a *gavur* (infidel) could marry her was by converting to Islam. Though he was from a devout Catholic family, the young man did not hesitate to change his faith. As a Moslem, he was given a ward in Macedonia, a town called Prilep, near Skopje. The couple moved there, had many children, and started first a vineyard, which was a failure, then a successful gunpowder business, the name of which became our family's, Barutçu (gunpowder makers).

This story was one of my favorites, and I made my grandmother tell it over and over again. I never profaned it by asking what language the old lady spoke who told the empress about Naime. My father, who was the family archivist, denied any truth to the story—although he had no explanation for the origins of great-great-grandmother Naime and her mysterious *dönme* (convert) husband in Prilep. Family records did not go back far enough, having been lost during the Macedonian wars, when surviving members of my grandmother's family left their estate in Prilep and fled to Istanbul. Is it genuine history? Or was my grandmother practicing the art of storytelling? The truth is as obscure as the life of Nakshedil herself.

We do know that Aimée DeBucq de Rivery was born in 1763 to a noble family in Martinique. Her cousin Josephine Tascher de la Pagerie married Napoleon Bonaparte. A legend tells of the two young girls going to a Creole fortune-teller in Pointe Royale, who predicted that they would both grow up to be queens, one to rule the East, the other the West.

In 1784, on her return to Martinique, after attending convent school in Nantes, Aimée was kidnapped by Barbarossa's corsairs. Twenty-one years old, Aimée was sold to the Dey of Algiers. Captivated by her beauty, the dey saw an opportunity to win the sultan's favor. He presented the girl to Abdulhamid I.

Aimée was fair, demure, and intelligent. The sultan named her Nakshedil (Embroidered on the Heart) and made her his favorite. She rose to the status of fourth kadin and found herself in the political crossfire of the harem: the first kadin, Nükhet Seza, and the second kadin, Mihrimah, were each trying to put their sons on the throne. Nakshedil observed, and she learned.

In 1789, the year of the French Revolution, Abdulhamid died. At the age of twenty-seven, Selim III became sultan. He asked Nakshedil to remain at the Seraglio harem with her son, Mahmud—his nephew. For Selim, Nakshedil was a personification of the France he had always admired. She became his confidante. She taught him French; and for the first time, a permanent ambassador was sent from Istanbul to Paris. Selim started a French newspaper and let Nakshedil decorate the palace in rococo style.

These Francophile reforms cost him his life. Selim was assassinated in 1807 by religious fanatics who disapproved of his liberalism. The assassins also sought to kill Mahmud, but Nakshedil saved her son by concealing him inside a furnace. Thus Mahmud became the next Sultan, accomplishing significant reforms in the empire that are, for the most part, attributed to the influence of his mother.

Although Aimée accepted Islam as part of the harem etiquette, she always remained a Christian in her heart. Her last wish was for a priest to perform the last rites. Her son did not deny her this: as Aimée lay dying, a Catholic priest passed—for the first time—through the Gates of Felicity and into the harem.

Jean-Léon Gérôme,
The Guard of the
Harem, 1859,
Oil on panel,
9½ x 5⅞ in.,
The Wallace
Collection, London

Eunuchs

One evening, I was leaving the house of a wealthy Mussulman, one of whose four wives was ill with heart disease; it was my third visit, and on coming away, as well as on entering, I was always preceded by a tall eunuch who called aloud the customary warning, 'Women, withdraw,' in order that ladies and female slaves might know that there was a man in the harem and keep out of sight. On reaching the courtyard the eunuch returned, leaving me to make my way out alone. On this occasion, just as I was about to open the door, I felt a light touch on my arm: turning around I found, standing close by me, another eunuch, a good-looking youth of eighteen or twenty, who stood gazing silently at me, his eyes filled with tears. Finding that he did not speak, I asked him what I could do for him. He hesitated a moment, and then, clasping my hand convulsively in both of his, he said in a hoarse voice, in which there was a ring of despair, 'Doctor, you know some remedy for every malady; tell me, is there none for mine?" I cannot express to you the effect those simple words produced upon me: I wanted to answer him, but my voice seemed to die away, and finally, not knowing what to do or say I pulled the door open and fled. But that night and for many nights after I kept seeing his face and hearing those mournful words; and I can tell you that more than once I could feel the tears rising at the recollection.

—Edmondo de Amicis, a young doctor of Pera, Constantinople *(1896)*

Süleyman Ağa

When I was a small child living in Izmir during the late forties, in a five-story house that was once the harem of a pasha, I knew a eunuch. His name was Süleyman Ağa, a gingerbread-colored man without hair on his face, so that he looked much younger than he was.

Süleyman Ağa always seemed to have a special gift just for me. I don't remember anymore what all these gifts were, except one. Once, when I was sitting on his lap, he pinched my pinkie between his own pudgy dark fingers and put on it a ring with a bright red stone. He put another ring on my ring finger, a dazzling one with a colorless stone. Next, my middle finger received another ring, this time with a green stone. He continued placing rings on all my fingers: on the index finger, one with a blue stone and on my thumb, a ring with a purple one. He brought each ring out of his pocket slowly, very slowly, each time showing his amusement, his eyes fixed on my face, observing my expressions. No one has since spoiled me to that degree.

Later, in the fifties, when we moved to Ankara, he continued to visit us now and then, always bringing a large box of cream-filled chocolates. My favorite was banana cream. (I hated the creme-de-menthe.) Although

With my parents at our house in Izmir, 1949

he came unannounced, often just as the family was sitting down to dinner, I was delighted to see him each time. I felt a leaping in my heart as I answered the door and saw his flaccid figure standing before me. My eyes immediately traveled to his hands, which held the most seductive chocolate box.

"Open sesame, open," he would say, his golden front teeth flashing at me, his voice pitched high—although I did not really know what that signified. But I did know that he seemed more like a woman than a man, in the way he slouched forward and caved in right around his belly, and in the softness of his face. He had an hourglass figure, and to me he felt like an old aunt.

In his absence, my parents referred to him as the *hadim,* or "eunuch." The word, my mother told me, meant "beardless"; some men were just that way. Another time I overheard my father saying that there weren't many of "them" left anymore, and when these die, the species will completely disappear from the country, and it will be the close of an embarrassing era.

I was about nine when the news came of his death.

Somewhere around that time, I found out that a eunuch meant a castrated man. And since I was not yet familiar with the details of male anatomy, I imagined a man with his penis cut off; it was a disturbing picture. I had passed the age of asking intimate questions of my parents, or anyone else, except for my close girlfriends, who did not seem to know much more than I. In history class, we did study about these castrated men from the days of the sultans. We learned how important they were and how they meddled in politics. Süleyman Ağa was one of the last.

Since then, I have seen re-creations of eunuchs in movies or dance or opera. They are often played by beautifully muscled, athletic, and semi-naked black men with gorgeous turbans and flashy daggers, but they are so unlike Süleyman Ağa that it is hard to imagine that the word *eunuch* describes both.

Origins

Even more than the sexual fantasies implicit in the harem, the eunuch commands utter fascination, as morbid as it is irresistible. I have not tried to resist here.

How did eunuchs come to be? Whose idea were they—and why? Clues lie in the things I have read, but it is all mostly speculative. The first traces of eunuchry appear in Mesopotamia, the cradle of civilization, where the rivers Tigris and Euphrates become one and empty into the Persian Gulf. In that delta, a beautiful valley nurtured many tribes—matriarchal societies among them. During the ninth century B.C., Semiramis, queen of Assyria, castrated male slaves. So did other queens. In *Voyage en Orient,* Gérard de Nerval describes a retinue of eunuchs who traveled with the Queen of Sheba (Saba).

Types of Eunuchs

History has known several kinds of eunuchs: congenital eunuchs, those castrated by other men, and those who chose castration for themselves as a means of achieving chastity. "For," as the Apostle Matthew declares (19:12), "there are eunuchs, which were so born from their mother's womb: and there are eunuchs, which were made eunuchs by men: and there are eunuchs, which made themselves eunuchs for the kingdom of heaven's sake."

The tradition of eunuchs traveled east, through Persia to China. Warring tribes, such as the Persians, castrated Ionian prisoners and offered them, along with the most beautiful virgins among the vanquished, to their kings. In 538 B.C., when Cyrus, King of Persia, captured Babylon, he proclaimed that since eunuchs were incapable of procreating and having their own families, they might be the most loyal of servants. As Xenophon, the ancient Greek historian and biographer (400 B.C), records:

> He drew this conclusion from the case of other animals: for instance, vicious horses when gelded, stop biting and prancing about, to be sure, but are none the less fit for service in war: and bulls, when castrated, lose part of their high spirit and unruliness but are not deprived of their strength, nor capacity for work. And in the same way dogs, when castrated, stop running away from their masters, but are no less useful for watching or hunting. And men, too, in the same way become gentler when deprived of this desire, but no less careful of that which is entrusted to them.

The Judeo-Christian notion of chastity and the perception of women as obstacles to achieving it encouraged castration. Tertullian, the second-century theologian, declared the Kingdom of Heaven open to eunuchs, encouraging many to castrate themselves.

Most who did regretted their decision.

Herodotus tells of a slave trader named Panionus from the island of Chios (Scio), infamous for his sexual practices. Panionus bought boys of extraordinary beauty, then castrated and sold them at the slave emporiums. One Hermotimus was among these. Years later, the paths of the slave trader and the eunuch crossed again. Hermotimus had acquired a great deal of power in Sardis as chief eunuch in a wealthy palace. He convinced Panionus to move there with his family, promising him power and wealth. Panionus, unaware of Hermotimus's hunger for revenge, agreed and moved his family into the palace—only to find himself overpowered by the eunuch, who forced him to castrate his four sons, and then forced the sons to castrate their father.

The Catholic Church had been castrating boys to preserve their soprano voices for the papal choir of the Sistine Chapel since the Renaissance—a practice that did not cease until 1878. In the eighteenth century, Italian opera favored *castrati* as well, some of whom became superstars, such as Grimaldi, Farinelli, and Nicolini.

Several hundred eunuchs were employed by the holy mosques of Islam in Mecca and Medina. Attendants had to come in contact with women who visited the mosques; such contact was not permissible between men and women in Islamic society, especially in a holy place. Therefore, the attendants had to be something less than men.

In the late eighteenth century, in Central Russia, a secret sect called the Skoptsi (from *skopets,* or eunuch) flourished. The Skoptsi believed in an unusual Garden of Eden myth, in which Adam and Eve had been created sexless. After the fall, however, sections of the forbidden fruit were grafted onto them as genitalia and breasts. In order to regain the pure, prelapsarian state, many willingly endured a castration ritual, often mutilating themselves with knives, sharp stones, even broken glass. Skoptsi still exist.

In Asia Minor, during the fifth century B.C., the priests of the Temple of Artemis in Ephesus (one of the seven wonders of the world) and the Temple of Sybelle were eunuchs. Later on, the sacred function of eunuchs changed into a form of luxury in Greece and in Rome. As Gibbon recounts: "Restrained by the severe edicts of Domitian and Nerva, cherished by the pride of Diocletian, reduced to a humble station by the prudence of Constantine, they mutiplied in the palaces of his degenerate sons, and insensibly acquired the knowledge, and at length the direction, of the secret councils of Constantius."

The custom lingered among the Byzantines and passed on to the Ottoman Turks. During the fourteenth century, when the Ottomans first began secluding their women, the Byzantines supplied them with eunuchs, but it did not take the Turks long to establish their own trade. In China, castration was already a well-established practice at this time, flourishing until the fall of the Great Palace of Peking. But while the eunuchs in China were all Chinese, in Turkey they were anything but Turks; for castration was forbidden in Islam. At first, then, the Turks acquired white eunuchs from conquered Christian areas such as Circassia, Georgia, and Armenia, but these eunuchs often proved fragile; mortality was high. Black eunuchs manifested more strength and better endurance. Egypt, Abyssinia, and the Sudan became lucrative hunting grounds.

Eunuch Trade

According to Islam, slaves captured in war become the property of their captor and, like all property, could be transferred. Moslem slave traders pursued certain African chiefs who willingly sold their people. Such transactions established a lucrative trade.

The majority of slaves came from the upper reaches of the Nile, from Kordofan, Darfur, Dongola, and near Lake Chad. They were shipped upriver to Alexandria or Cairo, packed spoon-fashion in boats; or from Darfur and Sennar in the Sudan, crossing the Sahara, partly on foot and partly on camels. Other slaves were transported from Abyssinia to the Red Sea ports and eventually to the greatest slave emporiums on the Mediterranean— Mecca, Medina, Beirut, Smyrna (Izmir), and Constantinople (Istanbul).

Procedures

Among the slaves, some young black boys were castrated on the way, at rest stops, by Egyptian Christians or Jews, since Islam prohibited the practice. It was a risky operation with a high mortality rate, and the hot, arid climate was not conducive to easy recovery. Desert sand was considered the most efficacious balm, so the newly castrated were buried up to their necks until their wound healed. The boys who survived the pain, hemorrhage, and subsequent burial became luxury items, bringing enormous profit to the traders. And since they attracted wealthy purchasers, the eunuchs' futures actually held opportunity for position and power.

A great deal of secrecy still surrounds the shady trade of eunuch-making, but the etymological history of terms associated with castration offers clues about the various procedures, which involved crushing, striking, cutting, and pulling.

During the Classical era, according to historian N. M. Penzer, the varieties of eunuchs were clearly defined:

Castrati, *clean-cut, both penis and testicles removed*
Spadones, *testicles removed by a method of dragging*
Thlibiae, *testicles bruised and crushed, the seminal glands permanently damaged—primarily performed on very young boys*

Sir Richard Burton, the famous traveler and Arabist, lists three similar types of castration practices in the Orient:

> *Sandali, or clean-cut. The genitals swept off by a single incision of a razor, a tube inserted into the urethra, the wound cauterized with boiling oil, and the patient planted in a fresh dung-hill. The diet is milk and, under puberty, survival rate high.*

> *Eunuch, whose penis is removed, still retaining the ability for copulation and procreation without the wherewithal.*

> *Eunuch, similar to* thlibiae, *rendered sexless by removing the testicles with a stone knife or by bruising, twisting or searing.*

The methods of castration seem to be universal around the world, except for variations in procedures for control of hemorrhage. Carter Stent describes how Chinese eunuchs were castrated (1877):

> *The operation is performed in this manner: white ligatures or bandages are bound tightly round the belly and the upper parts of the thighs, to prevent much hemorrhage. The parts to be operated on are then bathed three times with hot pepper-water, the intended eunuch being in a reclining position. When the parts have been sufficiently bathed, the whole—both testicles and penis—are cut off as closely as possible with a curved knife, in the shape of a sickle. The emasculation being effected, a pewter needle or spigot is carefully thrust into the main orifice at the root of the penis; the wound is then covered with paper saturated in cold water and carefully bound up. After the wound is dressed, the patient is made to walk around the room supported by two "knifers" for two or three hours, when he is allowed to lie down. The patient is not allowed to drink anything for three days, during which time he suffers great agony, not only from thirst, but from intense pain, and from the impossibility of relieving nature during that period. At the end of three days, the bandage is taken off, the spigot is pulled out, and the sufferer obtains relief in the copious flow of urine which spurts out like a fountain. If this takes place satisfactorily, the patient is considered out of danger and congratulated on it; but if the unfortunate wretch cannot make water, he is doomed to a death of agony, for the passages have become swollen and nothing can save him.*

The historian Paul Rycaut also describes eunuchs concealing a silver quill in their turbans; they inserted the quill into the urethra in order to urinate.

A prepubescent boy had the best chance of surviving the operation. After puberty, castration brought on a sense of irreparable loss and despair, mingled with frustration and longings for vengeance.

Chinese Eunuchs

The Forbidden City of Peking was almost exclusively male, and most of the inhabitants were eunuchs. During the Ming Dynasty (1368–1644), more than a thousand eunuchs lived within the walled city. Their number gradually dwindled, leaving only two hundred by the time of the last emperor Pu Yi's reign, at the beginning of the twentieth century. Although most of the eunuchs within the walled city performed menial tasks, great opportunities for promotion actually attracted the poor to the practice. Castration was an inexpensive operation with about a 4 to 5 percent mortality rate—a risk many considered worth taking. It was helpful for the novices to have connections within the walled city, since recruitment was under sponsorship by eunuchs already employed there.

Many eunuchs within the walls received a good education and were eventually employed as clerks. The ones with good singing voices acted in theatricals; others became confidantes of high officials. Since Confucian tradition required the burial of the whole body to attain heaven, they kept their sex organs in tiny jars full of brine, and carried them on their persons. A lucrative black market trade existed in these relics for those who were unable to preserve their own organs.

Effects of Castration

The physical effects of castration are lack of body hair, a falsetto voice, flabbiness, and obesity. Eunuchs also suffer from weak bladders, short memory, insomnia, and poor eyesight. Eunuchs learn to stay off alcohol because it dissipates their energy and causes pain in the urethra.

According to various accounts, harem eunuchs liked money and the things money could buy. They loved eating rich and sweet confections, like chocolate and pastries. They had an affinity for storytelling, savoring the wildest myths and fairy tales, especially those out of *One Thousand and One Nights*. They also enjoyed music and dance, which evoked the spirit of their native Africa: "Eunuchs and slaves went through the swaying measure of the dance, half hidden in clouds of burning spices and perfumes, which breezes from the Black Sea wafted over the entire Seraglio, and accompanied

Leon Bakst,
Eunuch. *Costume design for the Diaghilev ballet* Schéhérazade, *1910, Watercolor and gold on paper, Private collection*

by strains of barbaric warlike music," describes Edmondo de Amicis in *Constantinople* (1896).

Sexual Desire and Consummation

The loss of sexual organs does not seem to diminish sexual desire, especially if castration is performed at puberty, as the Roman satirist Juvenal observed: "The height of their enjoyment, however is when the lads have been led to the doctor in the heat and flush of youth with a bush of dark hairs already visible; and the testicles they have waited for and encouraged to grow in the early stages."

A eunuch who had lost only his testicles could still have erections and enjoy sex. Sir Richard Burton, in his voluminous translation of the *One Thousand and One Nights,* tells us that an erection could last as long as the heart kept pounding and passion remained intact. In "Tale of the First Eunuch," a black youth takes advantage of a girl and is punished by castration. Later, he becomes her eunuch and continues making love to her until her death.

Indeed, some eunuchs had passionate affairs with harem women. Montesquieu's *Persian Letters* evokes the suffering of an aroused eunuch:

> *When I entered the Seraglio, where everything filled me with regret for what I had lost, my agitation increased every moment, rage in my heart and despair unutterable in my soul. . . . I remember one day, as I attended a lady at the bath, I was so carried away that I lost command of myself and dared lay my hand where I should not. My first thought was that my last day had come. I was, however, fortunate enough to escape a dreadful death; but the fair one, whom I had made the witness of my weakness, extorted a heavy price for her silence: I entirely lost command of her, and she forced me, each time at the risk of my life, to comply with a thousand caprices.*

The eunuch who still had his penis was favored by harem women because of his ability to prolong his partner's pleasure. And potent eunuchs had an absolute corner on birth control.

Eunuchs sometimes kept their own odalisques, and others preferred young boys, as a court halberdier remarked in *Risale-i Taberdariye fi Ahzal-i Ağa'yi Darüssade* (1714):

> *These wretched men, they fall in love with handsome youths too and keep them close, these wretches have so much desire in their corrupt bodies. Every single one of them buys a couple of slave girls and secretly keeps them in their*

room, jealous of the others of their kind. They fight with each other over these women they keep in their rooms. How could a traitor commit such an act without sexual urge?

Eunuchs also experimented with aphrodisiacs and erotic paraphernalia. Having contact with the outside, they were able to obtain a variety of sex toys, including artificial phalli and other kinds of erotic succedanea. They were also highly skilled in the art of oral sex; a woman who married after having made love to eunuchs was often dissatisfied with her husband's performance, according to the halberdier:

> *Is it said that these odalisques who become intimate with eunuchs develop a voracious sexual appetite? That they do is a well-known fact all over Istanbul. Two odalisques were given their freedom and married off. A week after their weddings, the husbands divorced them. The reason being that the odalisques told their husbands they did not perform as well as the eunuchs. Because of that, the husbands divorced them. This incident occurred in my time.*

Eunuchs seem to have been quite unselfish in their sexual pursuits; therefore, we know less about the process of their own fulfillment, as they left us little discussion of it. Their erogenous zones were around the urethra and the anal cavity. Burton became acquainted with a eunuch's wife, who told him that her husband experimented with masturbation, fellatio, and anal sex until these acts induced a venereal orgasm from a secretion of the prostate gland. As he was about to climax, she would hold a pillow for him to bite. She was afraid that, in an unbearable fit of passion, he might have torn her breasts or face.

Marriage of Eunuchs

Marriages between eunuchs and odalisques in the Seraglio were not uncommon; but, once married, they lived outside of the harem. Sümbül Ağa, Ibrahim's chief eunuch, married a pregnant girl in order to have not only a wife but also a child to take care of. Many others filled harems of their own with virgins. "I was not looking for love, but for passion. I was unable to satisfy this irresistible desire in the palace," recorded a nineteenth-century chief black eunuch. "There were many women on whom I looked with desire, but I was deterred by visions of the gallows. Finally, I decided to get married. I married a woman who had come from the palace. You might ask how such a woman could marry such a man as I. I do not know. I never asked this once in all the years that we lived together."

In his *Diaries* (1699–1700), John Richards scorns with great disdain such marriage practices:

> *There is a sort of Marriage if it may be so called between a Eunuch and a Woman and I hear meane those who are cut close, notwithstanding it is credibly reported that they have commerce in a manner unknown to us, and it is no great matter, nay even the Women amongst themselves have ways of Supplying the Deffect of Men & it is not to be wondered att that these miserable Creatures who have no other knowledge themselves than that [they] are made for the use of Man, nor that faith which teaches a future reward and punishment for Vertue & Vice, it is not to be admired att, they should give themselves up to all manner of Lusts & Sensuality in which they say they excell all other Women.*

Regeneration of Genitals

Sometimes sexual organs grew back. Carter Stent records that after an investigation in a Chinese court, several eunuchs were discovered still endowed. They were immediately recastrated, but this time, being at a more vulnerable age, most did not survive.

A eunuch named Wei-chung-hsien, in the court of Peking, secretly kept a concubine and tried everything possible to regenerate his sexual organs. A doctor told him that if he ate the brains of seven men, he could retrieve his genitals. Wei-chung-hsien procured seven criminals, had their heads split open, the brains extracted from them, and devoured everything. We do not know the result.

Eunuchs were carefully scrutinized before admission to the Seraglio. Physicians examined them on arrival and checked them periodically to make certain that nothing had grown back. Also, eunuchs with unattractive faces were preferred; the beautiful, bejewelled, "blue" eunuchs were left to the pages of *One Thousand and One Nights*.

As many as six to eight hundred eunuchs were employed in the Seraglio at the height of the Ottoman Empire—mostly gifts from the governors of different provinces. Their living quarters were located immediately beyond the entrance to the harem, through the Gates of Felicity. The only entry was through two consecutive pairs of doors, one of iron, the other of brass. The chief eunuch received the keys every night from the watchman, the *baltacilar* (axe-man, or halberdier), and returned them in the morning.

John Frederick Lewis, Life in the Harem, Cairo, 1858, Watercolor and body color on paper, 23⅞ x 18¾ in., Victoria and Albert Museum, London

The anteroom still contains the bastinado sticks used on the newcomers. Each novice eunuch was subjected to the sticks, whether he deserved them or not. He would be stretched out on the floor, his hands and feet bound together, while an older eunuch hit his soles with the sticks for as long as the young boy could tolerate the pain. All the others were forced to observe and learn: "The boys are watched and disciplined by the other youths of the Seraglio, till at a certain age they are ready for service. They are then removed thence and sent to the women and placed under others in the service of the Sultana, being under the command of the Chief Eunuch, or head of the virgins. They get a considerable allowance, of 60 to 100 akcha a day, two robes of finest silk and other things throughout the year, besides what is plentifully bestowed upon them from other quarters. They bear names of flowers, such as Hyacinth, Narcissus, Rose and Carnation; since they are in the service of women they have names suitable to virginity, whiteness and fragrance," wrote Ottaviano Bon in *Seraglio of the Grand Signor* (1608).

They slept in a crowded dormitory while apprenticing with older eunuchs. They grew up, playing with other boys and child odalisques. The discipline of their training for the corps of eunuch guards was comparable to that in a military school. At the end of this training, like the odalisques, each was assigned to the service of a luminary in the harem—a prince, a kadin, a daughter or sister of the sultan, or the valide sultana. Their dream was to reach the status of the *kizlar ağasi* (master of the girls), the chief black eunuch.

The Chief Black Eunuch (Kizlar Ağasi)

The power and prestige of the kizlar agasi was tremendous. He was the highest-ranking officer in the empire, after the sultan and the grand vizier. He was the commander of the corps of baltaci, a pasha, and carried other illustrious titles. He could approach the sultan at any time and functioned as the private messenger between the sultan and the grand vizier. He had access to the valide sultana, as the liaison between the sultan and his mother. Any woman within the harem wanting to approach the sultan had to be screened by the chief black eunuch. He was an extremely wealthy man, greatly feared, and, consequently, the most bribed official in the whole Ottoman Empire.

He was the one who took a new odalisque to the Sultan's bedroom, a

*Two eunuchs in the
seraglio courtyard*

ceremony Jean-Claude Flachat describes in *Observations sur le commerce* (1766):

> *Finally the Saray Usta (Mistress of the House) presents to the sultan the girl
> which he finds most attractive. . . . She makes haste to display all her skills to
> please him. He throws a handkerchief to her as indication that he wishes to
> stay with her, and immediately the curtains around the room where he is sitting
> are drawn. The Kizlar Aga waits there for the signal to draw the curtains
> back, while all the other women who are dispersed here and there—some
> dancing, some singing, some playing musical instruments, and many resting—*

*enter the kiosk and present their respects to the sultan and their congratulations
to the new favorite.*

If any emergency occurred during the night, the kizlar ağasi was the
only person allowed to enter the harem. His duties were to protect the
women, provide the necessary odalisques for the harem, oversee the promotion of the women and the eunuchs, act as a witness for the sultan's
marriage and birth ceremonies, arrange all the royal ceremonial events, such
as circumcision parties, weddings, and fêtes, and deliver sentence to harem
women accused of crimes. He was the one who took the girls to the execu-
tioner, who had them put in sacks to be drowned.

In the second half of the sixteenth century, the power of the eunuchs
grew. In the seventeenth and eighteenth centuries, the eunuchs, like the
women, took advantage of child sultans and mentally incompetent ones to
gain political power. During the Reign of Women (1558–1687), the chief
black eunuch was the valide sultana's and the kadins' most intimate and
valued accomplice. Together, their role in the decline of the Ottoman Empire is significant:

> *Although it was said that forty of them did not have sufficient brains between
> them to fill a fig pip, the murders committed as a result of the influence wielded
> by these harem aghas were innumerable. During the reign of Abdulhamid,
> those who rose to the highest rank of* musahip *(gentleman-in-waiting to the
> sultan) were as powerful as the sultan himself. In the time of Abdulhamid, the
> Kizlar Agha frequently received the highest statesmen of the time in his rooms.
> One of the conspirators behind the March 31st tragedy was Jevher Agha. After
> the proclamation of Second Tanzimat the war office ordered his execution. My
> own experiences in the palace led me to divide the eunuchs into three different
> categories: the oversensitive, the foolish and the stupid. At the very mention of
> the word 'black' some would take umbrage. They would not drink coffee
> because it was black, instead they drank tea.*
>
>

Ali Seydi Bey, Teşrifat ve Teşkilatimiz
(Ceremony and Organization) *(1904)*

From the early nineteenth century until the fall of the empire, the power
of the chief eunuch declined. By the early twentieth century, his job was
simply to supervise the dress of the women, making sure that it was appropriate; to accompany the women in their outings and oversee their itiner-
aries, making certain that everything was conducted according to the rules;
to prohibit merchants, workers, and fortune-tellers from entering the harem

Discarded members of Sultan Abdülhamid's harem, with two eunuchs, on their way to Vienna to exhibit themselves; these women were unclaimed by relatives after harems were officially outlawed in 1909.

at will; to grant or deny permission to women visitors to enter or exit the harem; to leave after midnight; to be on call in case something critical happened after hours.

With the disappearance of harems, so expired the eunuchs. During their last days, there was a great deal of concern about their survival in old age. They feebly attempted forming unions. Nobody wanted to deal with them anymore, because they stood for a past everyone wanted to bury. "In the midst of a crowded bazaar," Edmondo de Amicis writes in *Constantinople* (1896), "among the throng of pleasure seekers at the Sweet Waters, beneath the columns of the mosques, beside the carriages, on the steamboats, in kayiks, at all the festivals, wherever people are assembled together, one sees those phantoms of men, these melancholy countenances, like a dark shadow thrown across every aspect of gay Oriental life."

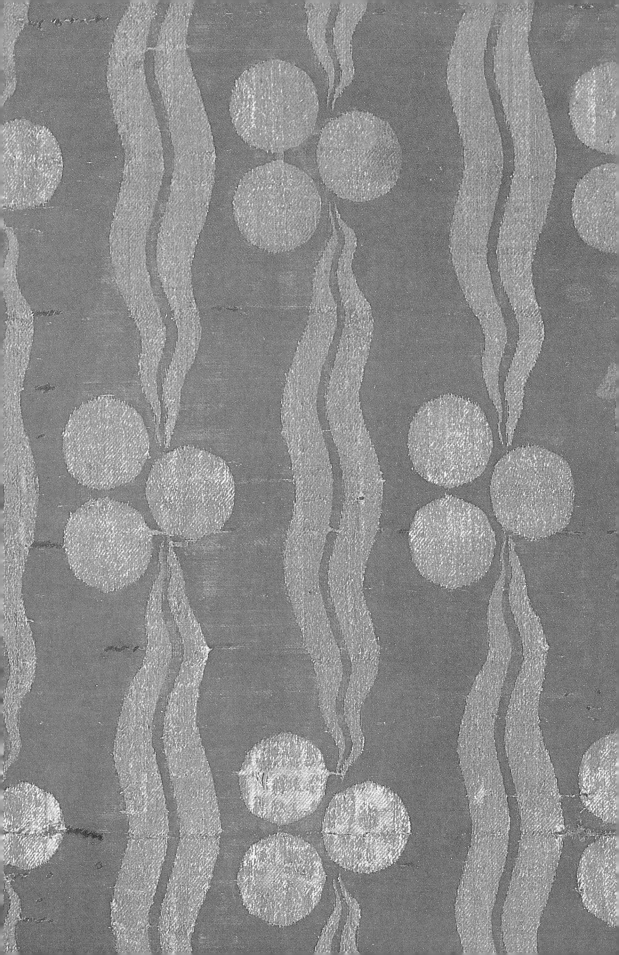

Harem Life in the City

Ordinary Harems

The Oriental woman is no more than a machine: she makes no distinction between one man and another man. Smoking, going to the baths, painting her eyelids and drinking coffee. Such is the circle of occupations within which her existence is confined. As for physical pleasure, it must be very slight, since the well-known button, the seat of same, is sliced off at an early age.
—Gustave Flaubert,
Letter to his mistress, Louise Colet (1850)

Harems were not exclusive to the Ottoman palaces. Prior to the twentieth century, women were segregated in almost every Moslem household in the Ottoman Empire—even in a few of the Christian and Jewish ones. While the wealthy lords kept opulent harems that were smaller versions of the Grand Harem, with numerous eunuchs and odalisques, the poor contented themselves with keeping two wives in one small room, a mere curtain separating them.

Unlike the sultans, ordinary Moslem citizens married daughters of other Moslem citizens. These women had been born into and stayed in their father's harems until they were married. Then they moved into their husband's harem, managed by the man's mother, the valide.

Marriages were arranged by families and each man allowed four legal wives, whom he was expected to keep in the same style and upon whom lavish equal affection; however, the first wife was considered the most important woman and often had greater legal privileges. In addition to the four wives, odalisques were available for purchase and brought into the harems as servants. It was not uncommon for the master to have sexual relationships with the odalisques as well. On rare occasions the men even married these servant women and legitimated their children.

*Edmund Dulac,
Illustration to
Quatrain LXXII of
The Rubaiyat of
Omar Kháyyám
(London: Hodder and
Stroughton, 1909),
Rare Book and
Manuscript Library,
Columbia University,
New York*

*Alas, that Spring
should vanish with
the Rose!
That Youth's sweet-
scented Manuscript
should close!*
. . . . .

The Go-Betweens

Since men and women did not associate socially, marriages were arranged by *görücü* (go-betweens), "agents" who visited harems, studied the merits of a certain girl, and passed their judgment on to the man's family. Sometimes these arrangements were orchestrated between relatives to strengthen the bonds of kinship. The betrothal of first cousins was and still is prevalent in most Islamic countries.

Henry T. Schafer,
The Bride, *ca. 1889,*
Photogravure,
7½ x 12½ in.,
Collection of the
author

Görücü were still operating during the sixties. Most of these women were self-proclaimed busybodies who prided themselves on their talent for matchmaking. They sought out pubescent girls for widowed, middle-aged, or unmarried men who seemed incapable of finding wives for themselves. Unannounced, the görücü appeared at a girl's house. Islamic custom not allowing one to turn away a guest, the girl's relatives would welcome the görücü—because that was their obligation. They served her coffee and sweets, acted polite, and made small talk. Meanwhile, the young girl would be hiding in the kitchen or in another room, until her mother or aunts invited her in. She would be required to make and serve Turkish coffee, since great importance was attached to her ability to brew this concoction. Her eyes cast down, she served the coffee to the görücü and her entourage, either leaving the room immediately after they had had sufficient opportunity to scrutinize her or sitting silently on the edge of her seat, listening to the other women carry on.

My friends and I used to make fun of this primitive custom, but since we were living in a country still caught in uneasy change, it was inevitable that we, too, would encounter the görücü. I recall on several occasions peeking behind the door and watching these women come for older girls in the family. I became very familiar with the ritual and antics. Barely after I had reached puberty, it was my turn. I was incensed at their gall and resisted coming out to meet them, but the older women in my family, steeped in the tradition, insisted that I present myself. In my rebellion, I did what I could to make myself unattractive, undesirable, and unwomanly—at least according to the prescribed standards. I dresssed inappropriately, made bad coffee, and talked too much. It was a great relief when they left, but often a source of quarrel, since my women relatives felt I had misbehaved, and I myself was humiliated by having been subjected to this archaic ritual. Although they sympathized with me—and it was always understood that I would find and choose my own husband—they felt hurt to see the age-old tradition crumble and realize that they were its last relics.

Romance

Despite the görücü and the arranged marriages, romance still smoldered in the imagination of young men and women. Pubescent girls, discovering their hearts for the first time, spent endless hours composing symbolic verses to imaginary handsome lovers. Thousands of small artifacts, such as flowers, fruits, blades of grass, feathers, and stones, were endowed with special meaning, usually expressed in a poem. A few cloves, a scrap of paper, a slice of pear, a bit of soap, a match, a piece of gold thread, a stick of cinnamon, and a corn of pepper signified "I have long loved you. I pant, languish, die with love for you. Give me a little hope. Do not reject me. Answer me with a word." The girls often got so carried away with their fantasy lovers that when their arranged husbands came along, heartbreak was inevitable.

For their part, young men were also romantics: "I could see that he was terribly in love, for with Arabs, a very little goes a long way; and never being allowed to see the young ladies, they fall in love merely through talking about them," observed Lady Anne Blunt in her 1878 journal.

Romance or not, families decided who married whom. My grandmother was promised to her father's best friend when she was merely a child. When they eventually got married, she was fourteen and my grandfather was forty.

Gifts

In the nineteenth century, if the husband-to-be came from a wealthy family, he would give his betrothed, as engagement presents, a silver mirror, perfumes, spice trays, pitchers of syrup, jam in crystal bowls, slippers stitched with golden thread for the fiancée, and slippers for the entire household fashioned according to the status of each.

The bride-to-be responded with chibuks inlaid with pearls, money and watch cases, an ablution set, towels embroidered with gold, and a silk apron.

Middle-class people presented more or less the same things but of lesser value, while men from the lower classes gave slippers to the bride-to-be and her mother, and finely ground coffee and sugar to the rest of the family.

Two common Eastern fantasies depicted on Iranian postcards: lovers served food and wine by a houri—an image that also symbolizes cennet (paradise) on earth—and a dying old man surrounded by a harem of houris.

Henna Night

One of the most quaint and enjoyable aspects of the wedding preparations was the henna night, which occurred on the evening before the wedding. Women spent the day at the hamam, bathing, grooming, luxuriating. At night, they gathered together in the same house and ceremoniously decorated the bride's hands, feet, and face with henna, then took turns applying it to one another. At the time of my childhood, henna nights had come to be considered a rural custom and were never practiced in the cities. But I do remember visiting relatives in the country and, for the first time, having both my hands covered with a gray-green paste that smelled like horse manure and that kept getting colder as the evening wore on. My hands next were wrapped up in cloth like twin mummies. I spent a restless night, incapacitated by my wrapped hands, yet so curious of the outcome that I did not dream of taking the bandages off. The next morning, one of the women carefully unwrapped my hands and washed off the hardened mud. Underneath, my fingers were bright orange. When I returned to the city, other children made fun of me. The henna did not come off for weeks, no matter how well I washed my hands.

Weddings

The bride and groom did not meet prior to the wedding. In his novel *The Disenchanted,* Pierre Loti dramatizes the unfairness of this situation: "During this last supreme day, still her own, she wanted to prepare herself as if for death, sort her papers, and a thousand little treasures, and, above all, burn things, burn them for fear of the unknown man who in a few hours would be her master. There was no haven of refuge for her distressful soul, and her terror and revolt increased as the day went on. . . . All these treasures, all the little secrets of beautiful, young women, their suppressed indignation, their vain laments—all turned to ashes, piled up and mingled in a copper brazier, the only Oriental object in the room."

The wedding ceremony began with the arrival of the bride at the groom's house, heavily veiled, often wearing a red wedding gown and an ornate tiara. She came through a silk tunnel stretched from the carriage to the front door. She was not allowed to look either to the right or to the left but had to keep her head straight while an older woman relative, usually an aunt, led her to a bridal throne on a dais. As she sat down, the women guests started trilling, and a drum-beating ritual began. The groom then entered, lifted the veil, and saw his bride's face for the first time. It was a crucial moment. He had the right to denounce her if what he saw was not pleasing to him. By throwing a handful of coins at the spectators, all of whom were women, he expressed his satisfaction and acceptance. The women made a wild dash for the money, squealing and elbowing each other. Many of these heavily veiled women were present at every wedding, and there were rumors about men shrouding themselves in women's guise just to catch a glimpse of the bride's face. Next the groom took the bride's hand, and together they went out of the room. Soon afterward, the groom left the house, not to see the bride again for the rest of the day. After his departure, a feast began—lasting the entire day; in wealthier households, sometimes several days. "It lasted forty days and forty nights" was the catch phrase that described the more opulent weddings.

Later that night the bride was delivered to the groom's bedroom by her male relatives. She entered the nuptial bed at the foot, lifting the bed covers in an elaborate ritual. She remembered that even in paradise, a wife's place was beneath the "soles of her husband's feet." And if that night her hymen did not bleed, the groom had again the right to get rid of her. Sheets with blood stains were displayed from the balconies to attest to a bride's virginity.

This was my grandmother's world, but it did not seem remote; and these tales were utterly terrifying. We heard many stories about disillusionment on such wedding nights, when a couple who had no previous contact were thrown into a most intimate encounter. My grandmother told us how shocked she was when my grandfather removed his turban and, underneath, had no hair. Since all the men in her own family—the only males she had come in contact with—possessed abundant hair, she had never seen a bald man. Her wedding night was spent in tears and hysteria. But they killed a rooster and smeared its blood on the sheets for all to see.

Husband-Wife Relationships

The singular duty of a married woman was to win her husband's approval and thereby redeem herself in this life and throughout eternity. The Koran declares: "The good wife has a chance of eternal happiness only if that is her husband's will. . . . The fortunate fair who has given pleasure to her master will have the privilege of appearing before him in paradise. Like the crescent moon, she will preserve all her youth and beauty until the end of time, and her husband will never look older or younger than thirty-one years."

*My great-uncle
Rüstem and his
odalisque/wife,
Pakize.*

Husbands and wives maintained a more or less formal relationship. Rules compounded rules in enforcing the separation that formed the basis of the harem. It was a man's privilege to look freely upon the faces of his wives, but if curiosity should take him any further, his eyes were accursed. Women did not offer companionship in a man's intellectual life or other interests. They belonged to his private world; they belonged in his harem. Women and men often dined separately. Men were forbidden not only to enter another man's harem but even to talk to other men about their own wives. It was sacrilegious—or *haram*—to make any reference to the female sex in public. Even in announcing the birth of a daughter, a man referred to "a veiled one," "a hidden one," or "a little stranger."

Polygamy

One of the slips of parchment that the Archangel Gabriel passed on to Mohammed said: "If your wives do not obey you, chastise them. If one wife does not suffice, take four." Mohammed himself had fifteen wives, an example that led to legalized abuse of the Koran's four-wife injunction.

According to the Koran, a woman's consent is not necessary for marriage. She can neither object to being one of four wives nor to her husband's having an unlimited number of odalisques. However, each of the four women must be treated with impartiality: each must have her own apartments, her own servants, and her own jewels.

In Turkey, before early twentieth-century reforms, four wives and odalisques were recognized by the Islamic law, but only the first wife was considered legal under civil law. She was the one married with the ceremony described above and she held more privileges above the other wives.

Although most men confessed to the temptation to have several wives, they found it less troublesome to have just one. An old Turkish proverb says: "A house with four wives, a ship in a storm." Indeed, women often competed for supremacy in the harems, which disturbed the happiness and peace of the entire household. "The wisest men preferred to enjoy a concubine episodically, or even to repudiate their wives, rather than harbour under the same roof the bitter rivalry of 'competing' wives," according to Nadia Tazi in her *Harems*. "And those who did decide to have several legal spouses eluded the troublesome side of harem life by maintaining various separate households in different districts of the city, among which they divided their time."

Good husbands were diplomats. They abided by the Koran and gave the impression of treating all of their women equally. If one got a new pair of gilded slippers, the others received the same. Often, all the womenfolk lived in one big, rambling house. If jealousy arose among the wives, the husband had to separate them into different households. "And," according to Gérard de Nerval, "if she does consent to live in the same house as another wife, she has the right to live entirely separately, and she does not take part with the slaves, as people imagine, in any delightful tableau, beneath the eye of the master and the spouse."

The husbands alternated nights in the bedrooms, spending Friday nights exclusively with their first wives. Indeed, K. Mikes, a Hungarian who lived in Gallipoli and Istanbul for forty-four years, notes in his collection of letters, *Turkiye Mektuplari* (1944–45), that first wives did have certain sexual rights: "If her husband neglects her for three consecutive Friday nights (this must be night joining Thursday to Friday) the wife can complain to the judge. If he neglects her for even longer, then she can obtain a divorce. This is rare, but *Shariat* (canonical law) permits it."

Relationships Among Wives

Most second and third marriages occurred during middle age and tended to be for pleasure. Men whose wives were barren or had passed the child-bearing age often sought young girls. Sometimes the older wife even persuaded her husband to take in a pubescent girl who could fulfill his desires and bear children. Vicariously, she relived her youth and passion, assuming responsibility as the head of the harem and finding additional wives for her husband, if necessary. One Western sojourner in Turkey found it difficult to believe that a wife could reconcile herself to such sharing of affection:

> The older wife had no children so she herself had chosen a wife for him young enough to be her daughter. . . . Both women were busy with preparations for the expected baby, to whom the first wife referred as 'our child' and she seemed to be as worried about the fate of her rival as she would have been about her daughter. Yet, who knows what sorrow was gnawing at her heart strings, for she loved 'the master'. Can one share the object of one's affections without a pang?
>
> Grace Ellyson, Turkey Today *(1928)*

Yet aging women were obliged to suppress such emotion. If they were no longer desirable or useful, there was no place for them to go. They needed to maintain their status in their husband's house at all costs, to do whatever they could to assure themselves a place to stay, even if it meant finding other women for their husbands.

> When he came in, he kissed his first wife first, then his second, and it seemed to me that there was a difference in his manner to the two, the first being that of a lover, the second that of an older man to a pet child.
>
> Demetra Vaka, Haremlik *(1909)*

We used to have a maid, a tiny, withered, birdlike creature with a beak nose and missing teeth. I think her name was Sherife Hanum. She was married to an attendant of my father's, and they had no children. I remember the old woman eyeing a laundry girl whom she later chose to be her *kuma* (literally, "rival"). The kuma bore to her husband three children the

A group of Algerian women arranged by a postcard photographer to evoke a harem scene, 1915

old woman called her own, and she worked her tired muscles to support her husband's wife and children. Women's emancipation in Turkey had officially abolished such institutions, but the attitudes of the people remained unchanged.

Still, it was humiliating for many women to live through this kind of ordeal. A great deal of anguish occupied women's hearts; they felt inadequate to please their husbands and fulfill their religious obligations. The following description of a home with two wives, written around 1909, comes from the able pen of the Turkish author Halide Edip:

When a woman suffers because of her husband's secret love affairs, the pain may be strong, but its quality is different. When a second wife enters her home and usurps half her power, she is a public martyr and considers herself an object of curiosity and pity. However humiliating this may be, the position gives a woman unquestioned prominence and isolation.

Whatever theories people may regard ideal as family constructions, there remains one irrefutable fact about the human heart, to whichever sex it may belong—it is almost organic in us to suffer when we have to share the object of our love, sexual or otherwise. As many degrees and forms of jealousy exist as human affection. But suppose time and conditioning were able to tone down this elemental feeling, the family problem still will not be solved. The nature and consequences of the suffering of a wife who in the same house shares a husband lawfully with a second wife and equal partner, differ both in kind and

degree from that of a woman who shares him with a temporary lover. In the former case, the suffering extends to children, servants and relations whose interests are themselves more or less antagonistic, and who are living in a destructive atmosphere of distrust and struggle for supremacy.

In my own childhood polygamy and its results produced a very ugly and distressing impression. The constant tension in our home made every simple family ceremony seem like physical pain, and the consequences of it hardly ever left me. The rooms of the wives were opposite each other and my father visited them in turn. When it was Teize's turn everyone in the house showed a tender sympathy to Abla, while when it was her turn no one heeded the obvious grief of Teize. She would leave the table with eyes full of tears, and one could be sure of finding her in her room crying or fainting. I remember very clearly my feeling of intense bitterness against polygamy. It was a curse, a poison which our unhappy household could not get out of the system.

I was so full of Teize's suffering and was so constantly haunted by her thin, pale face, tear stained and distorted with grief even when she was kneeling on her prayer rug, that this vision had become a barrier between me and Abla. Yet one emotion of sudden pity for Abla was just as natural to my heart as the other.

Huda Sharaawi, Egypt's revered feminist, was betrothed to her cousin in 1891, at the tender age of thirteen. The cousin was old enough to be her father and already had a slave concubine and children by her. Huda's mother made the groom sign an affidavit attesting that he would not take any more wives. Sensitive Huda was crushed by this marriage—from which, to her great relief, she was delivered after eighteen months, when her husband made another woman pregnant, thereby annulling the marriage.

Man's pleasure is like the noonday halt under the shady tree; it must not—it cannot—be prolonged.

Arab proverb

Huda's friend Attiya Saqqaf records in her memoirs (1879–1924) several breaches of confidence, when her husband, who often traveled, acquired more wives on the road—a common practice among "traveling men": "During the annual *haj* season he had worked on the pilgrim ships bound for Arabia. He would marry a woman aboard ship and divorce her upon arrival. His marriages were so numerous he couldn't count them nor did he know the number of children he had. Meanwhile, I found him going after servant girls in the house."

Sometimes men concealed from their first wife the fact that elsewhere they had another wife—sometimes even other children. When such a secret was discovered, the wife usually attempted to return to her father's house. Marianne Alireza tells how her brother-in-law kept another wife in Egypt, and when his first wife found out, she tried escaping to her family home—but was not able to get a driver to take her. For however disturbed a wife might be by the discovery of a secret wife, custom compelled her ultimately to take the revelation in stride. Paul Bowles, in his haunting novel *The Sheltering Sky,* describes a young American woman whose husband dies in

Pierre Auguste Renoir, Odalisque, 1870, Oil on canvas, 24¼ x 48¼ in., National Gallery of Art, Washington, D.C.; Chester Dale Collection

the desert while they are traveling. She is picked up by a caravan, and one of the leaders claims her as his own. He takes her back to his house, disguised as a boy so that his three wives will not feel threatened. He keeps "the boy" locked up in a tiny room he enters every afternoon to make wild love to her: "It would occur to her when he left and she lay alone in the evening, remembering the intensity and insistence of his ardor, that the three wives must certainly be suffering considerable neglect. . . . What she did not guess was that the three wives were not being neglected at all, and that even if such had been the case, and they believed a boy to be the cause of it, it never would occur to them to be jealous of him."

Mostly, harems housed extended families: wives, mothers, unmarried sisters and daughters, sometimes other distant women relatives who needed shelter. The wives, never knowing when the husband might visit the harem, kept themselves decked out in anticipation at all times. They always did their best to put on a cheerful, happy exterior and to conceal their anguish at all costs.

One of my aunts had a maid named Rabia. When Rabia was sixteen, she married a man who already had a wife. My parents talked about this disapprovingly. A few months later, Rabia returned. She had run away, she said, because the first wife and the mother-in-law had been torturing her. They made her slave away all day long, cleaning, cooking, and washing the laundry. She'd work so hard, she could not stay awake until the time her husband returned. But those awful women told her husband that she was lazy, stubborn, and good for nothing. All she did was sit around all day while they exhausted themselves.

Elizabeth Warnock Fernea, in *Guests of the Sheik,* describes a similar situation in an Iraqi village: " 'They hate me, they hide the sugar and steal my cigarettes, they pour salt into the food I prepare for my husband, they gossip about me to the neighbors and they tell my husband I am mean and will not help with the housework. They want nothing except to get me out. How can I make friends with them?' She broke down and sobbed loudly in her *abayah* [long veil]."

Superstition and Charms

Women resorted to numerous superstitious practices in order to assuage their anguish. They dissipated their jewels and other worldly goods among the gypsies, herbalists, and *jadis* (witches), buying concoctions to make their rivals barren and to prevent their husbands from desiring other women. Gypsies read palms, coffee grounds, or beads. They gave talismans to women to preserve their youth, or decoctions to make a love philter, or a fetish to make cruel husbands kind, or evil-eye charms to protect children. It was considered a bad omen to say good things about a child's health and growth because that was tantamount to inviting the evil eye, so women looked at each other's children and said, "poor thing."

I remember a tinker who lived near us in Karshiyaka. His wife, Dudu, was an enormous woman with a bad temper. She especially disliked children. She threw stones when she saw us picking pine nuts from the cones, even though the trees did not belong to her. Everyone gossiped about how the poor tinker, a mild-mannered man, should find another wife—especially since Dudu could not even bear him children. One summer, the rumor was that the tinker indeed had eyes for another woman, a young widow with a little boy. Everyone thought this would be a good match; it would not only offer him a pleasant woman who could bear children, but also provide a home for her orphaned son.

We did not see Dudu for days, even when we picked pine nuts behind her house. Rumor said she had gone to see a witch woman.

One day, as my friend Esin and I were playing in a field, we saw Dudu walking at a very fast pace down the road, carrying a live rooster upside down, which kept pecking at her hands and flapping its wings. After she went into her house, we hid behind the fence to watch her. She came back out of the house, carrying the rooster, a basin of water, and a kitchen knife. She immersed the bird's neck in the water and struck the jugular. The bird blissfully bled to death in the water.

A few days later, the young widow's son was diagnosed as having meningitis. He did not live very long. It was the rooster that did it, they said. It was charmed. The widow left town, and the poor tinker was stuck with nasty, shrewd Dudu.

Upkeep

In some ways, harems were like growing businesses. More wives were brought in as the maintenance of a household became more complex and demanded more attention. There were children to take care of, servants to supervise, guests to entertain. New blood was needed to perform some of these tasks. So the harems grew. De Nerval compares them to a sort of convent: "When there are many women, which only happens in the case of people of position, the harem is a kind of convent governed by rigid rule. Its main occupation is bringing up children and the direction of the slaves in the household work. A visit from the husband is a ceremonial affair, as is that of close relatives, and as he does not take his meals with his wives, all he can do to pass the time is to smoke his nargileh seriously, and drink coffee or sherbets. It is the proper thing for him to give notice of his coming in advance."

"They do not, as the common description of *harem* life leads us to believe," comments historian C. B. Kluzinger (1878), "recline the live-long day on a soft divan enjoying *dolce far niente,* adorned with gold and jewels, smoking and supporting upon the yielding pillow those arms that indolence

Osman Hamdi, Girl Arranging Flowers in a Vase, 1881, Oil on canvas, 57 x 38 in., Istanbul Resim ve Heykel Müzesi (Istanbul Painting and Sculpture Museum). Osman Hamdi was a Turkish painter who studied in Paris under Gérôme.

makes so plump, while eunuchs and female slaves stand before them watching their every sign, and anxious to spare them the slightest movement."

Odalisques

Besides the wives, the men had the odalisques to reckon with. Odalisques had no rights at all until they were married, and even marriage freed them only from being outright slaves; they were now the property of their husbands. My great uncle Rüstem had an odalisque, a beautiful woman named Pakize, who served him as his wife until he died. Even though, for all

Sir Frank Dicksee,
Leila, *1892*,
Oil on canvas,
The Fine Art
Society, London

Achille-Jacques-Jean-
Marie Devéria,
Odalisque, *1810*,
Oil on canvas,
9 x 12½ in.,
Norton Simon Art
Foundation,
Pasadena, California

practical purposes, she *was* his wife, the rest of the women, the "legitimates," were prejudiced against her and looked upon her as a servant.

In large households, where several male family members shared the *selamlik* (the men's section), the odalisques had a more difficult plight. A carnival troupe who used to perform in Izmir during my childhood had a popular song, which they sang to the tune of "Baa, Baa, Black Sheep," about a slave girl who became pregnant and was called before the family to tell who, among the masters of the big household, was the father. "Tell us who, tell us who?" sang a chorus of men. "I cannot, I cannot, for I don't know who," responded the girl. "Tell us who, tell us who, don't be afraid to." After a long pause, the girl coquettishly began singing, "Well, there was old master so and so and the young one, too. And the older brother of the master, and the brother of the mistress . . ." and so on.

All the slave women in the house were at the disposal of the master. The children born of these slaves were considered legitimate, and the woman rose to the rank of wife. Leyla Saz summarizes the precarious position of the odalisques:

> The odalisques who were favorites of the master of the household or who had borne children, had one or two rooms each. However, if their master became tired of them, two or three of them were cluttered into one room, their status even lower than a black slave, who could at least be in the master's presence. These unfortunates were terrified to meet the heartless man, and spent their lives fawning upon his mistress, trying to quench their pangs of jealousy.

Even worse, it was quite simple to get rid of unwanted wives or odalisques with perfect impunity; for no man, not even a police inspector, could enter another's harem.

Jewelry

A woman's jewelry was her only insurance against disaster; legal action could be taken against any man who attempted to seize a woman's gold or gems.

When my grandmother was widowed, she sold all her jewelry, little by little, to put her sons through school. Sometimes with tears in her eyes she would describe an emerald necklace with thousands of tiny baby pearls, which she had inherited from her own grandmother. "But it's all right, it's all right, because it bought this house." She was referring to the house in the Karatash section of Izmir, where I was born. To a child's mind, used to judging the value of things by their size, it was incomprehensible that a necklace could actually buy an entire house.

Living Quarters

The windows of the women's apartments either opened onto an inner court-yard or were closely barred with latticework, concealing them from the outside world. These artfully designed, intricately woven lattices are some of the most beautiful elements of Islamic architecture, but what made them most compelling were the silhouettes of the shadows behind them, intimating a thousand and one mysteries and intrigues. "Almost all the rooms are small," according to Edmondo de Amicis's *Constantinople* (1896), "the floors covered with Chinese matting or rugs, screens painted with flowers and fruits, a wide divan runs all around the wall, pots of flowers stand on the window sills, there is a copper brazier in the center, and lattices cover the windows. In the Selamlik, the men's section of the household, a man works, eats, receives his friends, takes his siesta, and sometimes sleeps at night. The wives are never allowed to enter. Although it is separated from the harem simply by a narrow corridor, it is like two separate houses. Often different servants serve the two sections and there are separate kitchens."

Enclosed balconies with latticed windows allowed women to observe what was going on outside without being seen. Courtyards, roof gazebos, and gardens gave them a chance for a breath of fresh air, though these places were still considered *haram*. Roof terraces were favorite places to watch the boats go by, take a siesta, and enjoy refreshments. They also allowed women to go unnoticed from one house to another.

Women in harems frequently visited each other, bringing gossip, un-usual recipes, embroideries, and showing off their new dresses and jewelry. Often these visits were unannounced. If the husband found slippers at the entrance to the harem, it was an indication that the wives were entertaining guests and he was not supposed to go in. Such guests often stayed on for several days.

In our house in Istanbul, two very old spinsters lived on the first floor. They were sisters, neither of whom had married because their father had wanted to keep them for himself. Their youth had been spent behind harem lattices, which they still imposed upon themselves in order to perpetuate existence in a murky shadow world. They had jalousie shades put up to bar themselves from the vision of those who passed by and to watch the world parade before them without being seen. Whenever I walked down the stairs

Jean-Joseph Benjamin-Constant, A Morocco Terrace, Evening, 1879, Oil on canvas, 48½ x 78⅛ in., The Montreal Museum of Fine Arts; Gift of Lord Strathcona and his Family. Women relax on roof terraces, concealed from the rest of the world but able to observe it from a distance.

to go out the front door we shared, I could hear their footsteps padding to the windows, where they would situate themselves at a vantage behind the shutters from which to observe me. They seemed to experience vicarious pleasure in ogling the innocence of youth. They also seemed to be seeking any sign of scandal they could turn to gossip.

Gérard de Nerval discussed the harem of a sheik—with the sheik himself:

> *The arrangement of a harem is the same. . . . There are always a number of little rooms surrounding the large halls. There are divans everywhere, and the only furniture consists of tortoiseshell tables. Little arches cut into the wainscoting hold narghiles, vases of flowers, and coffee cups.*
>
> *The only thing which these harems, even the most princely of them, seem to lack, is a bed.*
>
> *"Where do they sleep, these women and their slaves?" I asked the sheik.*
> *"On the divans."*
> *"But they have no coverlets?"*
> *"They sleep fully dressed. But there are woollen or silken covers for the wintertime."*

"*That is all very well, but where is the husband's place?*"

"*Oh, the husband sleeps in his room and the women in theirs, and the odalisques on the divans in the larger rooms. If the divans and the cushions don't make a comfortable bed, mattresses are put down in the middle of the room, and they sleep there.*"

"*Fully dressed?*"

"*Always, but only in the most simple of clothes, trousers, vest and robe. The law forbids men as well as women to uncover themselves before the other sex, anywhere below the neck.*"

"*I can understand,*" I said, "*that the husband does not greatly care to pass the night in a room filled with women fully dressed, and that he is ready enough to sleep in his own; but if he takes two or three of these ladies with him . . .*"

Balthus,
La Chambre
Turque, *1963,*
Oil on canvas,
70⅞ x 82⅝ in.,
Musée National d'Art
Moderne, Centre
Georges Pompidou,
Paris

Below:
Eugène Delacroix,
Women of Algiers
in Their Room, *1834,*
Oil on canvas,
71 x 90¼ in.,
Musée du Louvre,
Paris

165

A woman plays ud *in
a real Turkish harem.
At the turn of the
century the harems
were decorated in
Oriental style mixed
with European Art
Nouveau.*

*Nineteenth-century
commercial
photograph of a
woman in harem dress*

"Two or three!" cried the sheik indignantly. "What dogs do you imagine would act in such a way? God alive! Is there a woman in the world, even an infidel, who would consent to share her honorable couch with another? Is that how they behave in Europe?"

"In Europe," I replied, "certainly not; but the Christians have only one wife, and they imagine that the Turks, who have several, live with them as with one only."

"If there were Mussulmans so depraved as to act as the Christians imagine, their lawful wives would immediately demand a divorce, and even their slaves would have the right to leave them."

Bundle Women

European merchants sometimes married local Christian women so that they could infiltrate the harems with their merchandise. Marianne Alireza describes such an encounter: "I guessed that she was some poor soul who had come for a handout and that the bundles contained our contribution. But she was a lady peddler and the bundles contained her wares. She was Circassian and had come many years before to perform the pilgrimage and like so many others decided to stay. Her goods were mostly notions and cheap toys, some bangles and trinkets, and a *buksha* with cheap gaudy fabrics and some lace. From a sheer need for some kind of excitement, women of the harem purchased almost everything."

Bundle women often appeared at our doorstep, and I cannot forget my excitement and wonder as I watched their wares slip out of the bundles. They were strange things, bedspreads of garish colors and tasteless baroque designs from Damascus, diaphanous nightgowns made of Shile fabric, and a profusion of lace and ribbons. My grandmother and my mother always bought something for my hope chest, which, I must have known deep down, represented not my needs but an excuse for my mother and grandmother to enjoy buying odd things. Over the years, the hope chest dwindled, the bedspreads and those ethereal nightgowns given away as gifts to women relatives who got married or servants who had been good to the family.

"Alev's hope chest" was still in my parents' house when I last visited them. Inside, there were just a very few things: some doilies, scarves, and the Damascus bedspread I remembered buying from a bundle woman. My mother insisted that I take it back with me, and I was caught between wanting to please her and being appalled by the wild bright orange, yellow,

A harem lady visited by a bundle woman and a gypsy fortune-teller: precious contact with the outside world. Collection of the author

and green florals. It would never do. But I took it with me anyway, slightly embarrassed when Turkish customs searched my suitcase and this particular artifact was questioned. Was it an antique? Did I have special permission from the government to export it? I told them it was a gift from the family, and that it had been in my family ever since I could remember. Why was I going through such an ordeal for something I was embarrassed by and would give to the Goodwill as soon as I returned home? (It turned out that a friend, who happened by while I was unpacking, fell in love with this ungodly piece of "art," and it now adorns her bedroom in San Francisco.)

Again, during the same visit, I was sitting in a cafe in the Prince Islands, surrounded by a bevy of Arab harem women, waiting for the ferry, when a Circassian woman came through the crowd, carrying two suitcases, which in today's world had replaced the old "bundle." She spilled open her suitcases for the women and could not escape my own curious eyes as she held up her wares for them to see. I was disappointed that the exotics I remembered were gone; no more strange kaftans, Damask silks, Jerusalem cottons. Now the bundle woman was selling mainly crochet and knit items made from synthetic yarns, which are ever so popular today in the Middle East, and there were some cheap Turkish towels and *bornozes* (bathrobes) from the tourist loom. The romance of the real bundle ladies was over.

Death

The dead were washed, shrouded, and buried as soon as possible. Coffins were not used because the Moslems believe that the body must be returned directly to the earth. There was no group service over the body, but for forty days the family was expected to open their door to the public, who would visit and pay condolences. Coffee, tea, and other refreshments were served to the visitors, and fresh waves of grief had to be shared with each arrival. A special halvah made of farina, cinnamon, and nuts—which is delicious—was also served; it represents the dead person's body. On the fortieth day, a professional chanter intoned verses from the Koran, and the women covered their heads, prayed, and sent the spirit of the departed away.

Whether the deceased was a man or a woman could be determined from the shape and decoration of the tombstone; women's headstones had flower designs and men's were shaped like turbans.

> *Every Friday, which is the day of religious observance for the believer, a long line of veiled women accompanied by children wends its way along the cemetery road, like a row of reeds along a river. The women love the cemetery: for them it means temporary reprieve from the generally cloistered condition imposed on them by the laws of Islam; it represents a destination for an outing; and the tears they shed for the departed provide relief for their worries.*
>
> *Etienne Dinet,* Tableaux de la vie arabe *(1908)*

West Meets East

Oriental Dream

It is a world in which all the senses feast riotously upon sights and sounds and perfumes; upon fruit and flowers and jewels, upon wines and sweets, and upon yielding flesh, both male and female, whose beauty is incomparable. It is a world of heroic, amorous encounters. . . . Romance lurks behind every shuttered window; every veiled glance begets an intrigue; and in every servant's hand nestles a scented note granting a speedy rendezvous. . . . It's a world in which no aspiration is so mad as to be unrealizable, and no day proof of what the next day may be. A world in which apes may rival men, and a butcher may win the hand of a king's daughter; a world in which palaces are made of diamonds, and thrones cut from single rubies. It's a world in which all the distressingly ineluctable rules of daily living are gloriously suspended; from which individual responsibility is delightfully absent. It is the world of a legendary Damascus, a legendary Cairo, and a legendary Constantinople. . . . In short, it is the world of eternal fairy-tale—and there is no resisting its enchantment."

—B. R. Redman, *Introduction to*
The Arabian Nights Entertainments *(1932)*

Henry William Pickersgill, Portrait of James Silk Buckingham and His Wife, *1816, Oil on canvas, 60¼ x 48 in., Royal Geographical Society, London. Buckingham, a journalist who traveled extensively in the Orient, poses in Oriental costume with his wife, Elizabeth.*

In German there is a beautiful word for the East, *Morgenland,* the land of the morning. The East, or the Orient, is where the sun comes from, and it encompasses Asia Minor, Persia, Egypt, Arabia, and India.

Orientalism is the Western version of the Orient, created by the Western imagination and expressed by Western art forms. It is the East of fantasy, of dreams. In fact, most Orientalist artists merely dreamed; they created their visions of the Orient without ever leaving their home country. A few, however, actually traveled to the East, daring to temper fantasy with fact. But even these adventurers could not resist the temptation to inflate their visions with a romantic breath, as Julia Pardoe observed as early as 1839: "The European mind has become so imbued with ideas of Oriental mysteriousness, mysticism and magnificence, and it has been so long accustomed to pillow its faith on the marvels and metaphors of tourists, that it is to be doubted whether it will willingly cast off its old associations and suffer itself to be undeceived."

One Thousand and One Nights

During the early eighteenth century, the floodgate of romance was opened —not as a result of politics or commerce, but by a book of fairy tales. In 1704, a French scholar named Antoine Galland translated *Alf Laila wa Laila,* the *One Thousand and One Nights,* or *Arabian Nights.* These tales were set in the kingdom of the great caliph Harun al Rachid, inhabited by mysterious sultans, eunuchs, and slave women, as well as genies, giants, and pegasi (flying horses). When Sultan Shahriar discovers that his wife has been unfaithful to him, he executes her, declaring that all women are as evil as the sultana and the fewer the world contained, the better. Every evening, he marries a new wife just to have her strangled the following morning. It is the job of the grand vizier to provide the sultan with these unfortunate girls from a terrorized kingdom. One day, the grand vizier's daughter, Scheherazade, who clearly has a scheme, persuades her father to take her to the sultan as his new wife:

> When the usual hour arrived, the Grand Vizier accompanied Scheherazade to the palace, and left her alone with the Sultan, who bade her raise her veil and was amazed at her beauty. But seeing her eyes full of tears, he asked what was the matter.
>
> "Sire," replied Scheherazade, "I have a sister who loves me tenderly as I love her. Grant me the favor of allowing her to sleep this night in the same room, as it is the last we shall be together."
>
> The Sultan consented to this petition and Dinarzade was sent for. An hour before the daybreak Dinarzade awoke, and exclaimed as she had promised:
>
> "My dear sister, if you are not alseep, tell me I pray you, before the sun rises, one of your charming stories. It is the last time I shall have the pleasure of hearing you."
>
> Scheherazade did not answer, but turned to the Sultan:
>
> "Will your highness permit me to do as my sister asks?" said she.
>
> "Willingly," he answered.
>
> So Scheherazade began . . .

Sultan Shariar is so captivated by Scheherazade's tales that he spares her life on condition that she will tell him more. Thus, the beautiful sultana fills one thousand nights and a night with romance. Scheherazade spins one captivating tale after another, one night after another, redeeming her life. The sultan's attitude toward women is transformed, the kingdom is healed, and everyone lives happily ever after.

Edmund Dulac,
Schéhérazade.
*Original watercolor
for frontispiece of*
The Thousand and
One Nights, *1907,
Watercolor on paper,
13⅝ x 6⅝ in.,
Jo Ann Reisler, Ltd.,
Vienna, Virginia*

    As folk tales, these stories were singular to begin with, but, in time, evolved into a Chinese-box pattern of tales within tales within tales. They metamorphosed as they traveled, but never lost the element of dangerous exoticism, implications of hidden mysteries, and erotic nuances. Their plots are utterly convoluted mirrors within mirrors. One of Horace Walpole's celebrated letters (to Mary Berry, August 30, 1789) suggests the appeal the tales held even for an eighteenth-century man of letters; "I do not think the Sultaness's narratives very natural or very probable, but there is wildness in them that captivates."

A man enjoying himself with more than one woman was a compelling fantasy, and Galland was a gifted storyteller. The tales themselves were very seductive, quickly becoming a sensational form of popular adult entertainment in Europe. They also partook of what nowadays we might call the "expansion of consciousness." Bored with the already established contexts, many writers found refuge in these Eastern labyrinths for their own tales, always sustaining elements from the original.

Edouard Manet, Olympia, 1863, Oil on canvas, 51 x 73¾ in., Musée d'Orsay, Paris

Wind From the East

One Thousand and One Nights not only introduced to Europe a new art of storytelling, but also provided a theatrical arena for a flamboyant society. Eighteenth-century men and women loved to dress up and play, and with *The Arabian Nights,* their repertory grew, giving them a new set of archetypal characters to impersonate.

In Paris, *Turqueries* became the rage, influencing everything, from theater, opera, painting, and romantic literature to costume and interior design.

Harem pants, satin slippers, and turbans became faddish items of high fashion. Nobility dressed like pashas, odalisques, sultanas; they posed in Turkish costumes for portraits by the popular painters of the period. Many dabbled in imitations of Eastern poetry. Women indulged in telling stories *à la* Scheherazade.

Nargilehs, low divans, and jeweled scimitars gradually insinuated their way out of the chic houses and into more prosaic dwellings throughout Europe. The concept of *keyf* (fulfillment in sweet nothingness)—*dolce far niente*—spread as a popular philosophy among Europeans, who were developing a penchant for quiet euphoria. Smoking opium and hashish became an aesthetic and spiritual pursuit used to expand the creative romantic mind. Poets and writers like Coleridge and De Quincey indulged in opiates to induce prophetic visions, giving voice to such sensuous masterpieces as "Kubla Khan," which Coleridge wrote while under the influence. Gérard de Nerval, Eugène Fromentin, Théophile Gautier, and Charles Baudelaire gathered in the Hôtel Pimodan, where members of the Club des Haschichins held secret smoking salons.

France was setting a trend for adapting Oriental tales into social satire. Voltaire wrote *Zadig;* Montesquieu, *Persian Letters;* and Racine, *Bejazit,* dramatizing a terrible struggle between two sultanas, modeled on the lives of Kösem and Turhan, and presenting in the process a metaphor for the repression of desire in eighteenth-century Western society. The play was enthusiastically received by a public who saw in it their own secret passions come to life.

Simultaneously, musical harems filled the palaces of Versailles and the Hapsburg court. During the late eighteenth century, Mozart introduced visions of a salubrious Orient in *The Magic Flute,* whereas *Abduction from the Seraglio* had been smashingly exuberant in its exoticism and presentation of virtuous Oriental humanity—music and dance coming to the rescue of a beautiful odalisque in the Seraglio. Into the early nineteenth century, other compositions, Bauldieu's *Caliph of Bagdad,* "Mameluke's Waltz," Beethoven's "Turkish March," and other Turkish marches followed, finding ultimate Orientalist expression in Rimsky-Korsakoff's *Scheherazade.*

"It was like a scene out of the *Arabian Nights*" became the cliché phrase used to describe any amazing, rich, or peculiar experience. Out of lassitude or otherwise, the well of Western culture seemed to be running dry, which made the pursuit of the exotic irresistible. Tourism to the East boomed. The Orient beckoned to many Westerners. As Rudyard Kipling said: "Once you have heard the call of the East, you will never hear anything else."

Lady Mary Montagu

"The world here Romantic. Women differ from ours. Unaffected. Lazy life," wrote Lady Mary Wortley Montagu to Alexander Pope from Istanbul. Between 1716 and 1718, she lived in Turkey as the wife of the British ambassador, Edward Wortley Montagu. One of the first great romantic women travelers to the Orient, she was full of self-discovery, incessantly writing her impressions and carrying on a fastidious correspondence with her European friends. Her *Turkish Embassy Letters* are perhaps the most authentic and direct experience of the East any *gavur* (infidel—also, foreigner) has articulated.

Lady Mary radiated all the eighteenth-century contradictions that Orientalism revealed. She was caught in the creative tensions between passion and reason, love of romance and pragmatism, a spirit of adventure and a rage for order. She surrendered to the seduction of the East, while maintaining her identity as a young English noblewoman. Her year in Istanbul, where "luxury was the steward and treasure inexhaustible," was extraordinary. She achieved the ultimate fantasy of entering the harem, the most forbidden part of the Islamic world. For the first time, we have a Western woman's direct experience of this world. Her descriptions of women in harems are beautiful, lush and opulent: "On a sofa rais'd 3 steps and cover'd with fine Persian carpets sat the Kahya's lady, leaning on cushions of white satin embroider'd, and at her feet sat 2 young Girls, the eldest about 12 years old, lovely as Angels, dress'd perfectly rich and almost cover'd with Jewells. . . . I must own that I never saw any thing so gloriously Beautifull," she wrote to her sister, Lady Mar, on April 18, 1717.

She was the perfect voyeur; the sensuality of such scenes did not elude her. At the same time, she remained faithful to her own cultural identity and sense of propriety. For example, when she was asked to join a few ladies in the baths and realized that they were all "stark naked," she was able to demur through convenient dissembling: "I was at last forced to open my shirt and show them my stays, which satisfied them very well, for I saw they believed that I was locked up in that machine, and that it was not in my power to open it, which contrivance they attributed to my husband."

She carried on an intimate correspondence with the poet Alexander Pope, in which they collaborated on the creation of an Orientalist world. Lady Mary actually experienced this world; Pope fantasized vicariously: "I have detested the Sound of honest Woman, and loving Spouse ever since I heard the pretty name of Odalisque," Pope wrote to Lady Mary on Septem-

*Attributed to J. B.
Vanmour,*
Lady Mary
Montagu with Her
Son and Attendants,
*ca. 1717, Oil on
canvas, 27 x 35½ in.,
National Portrait
Gallery, London*

ber 1, 1718. Like other men of this period, he went as far as to put in an order for a Circassian slave woman: "This is really what I wish from my soul, tho it would ruin the best project I ever lay'd, that of obtaining, thro' your means, my fair Circassian Slave."

Lady Mary did not import a slave for the hunchbacked poet, but she did bring back a great many *turqueries* to England, including harem attire, which soon became chic. She innoculated her children with smallpox vaccine, as she had seen done in Turkey, some seventy years before Dr. Edward Jenner "introduced" vaccination to England. Voltaire, who was familiar with Lady Mary's practices, attributed the origins of this vaccine to the Circassian women, who were highly esteemed in harems. They wished to avoid smallpox in order to preserve their beauty from pockmarks.

In the visual arts, harem scenes had, by the nineteenth century, become a convenient excuse for painting titillating nudes. The odalisque had become the symbol of exotic and erotic splendor. Ingres's *The Great Odalisque* (1814) was utterly unoriental in its cool classicism, depicting an elongated, reclining woman, resembling an alabaster urn, in an atmosphere of utter sensuous mystery. A vessel herself, impenetrable. The artist had merely transformed a nude woman into an Oriental phantasm by adding a turban, a fan, and a nargileh. Paris was flooded with a glut of Orientalist paintings, the success of which finally led to the establishment of the Salon des Peintres Orientalistes Français in 1893.

Jean-Auguste Dominique Ingres, La Grande Odalisque, *1814, Oil on canvas, 35¾ x 63¾ in., Musée du Louvre, Paris*

Journey to the Orient

For most nineteenth-century Westerners, everyday realism was too vulgar to be presented as art. In search of suitable subjects, then, many artists traveled to the East, which had remained virtually unchanged since Biblical times. The gradual improvement in transportation and better accommodations made the lands of the East increasingly accessible, and by 1868 Thomas Cook had established tours up the Nile and into the Holy Land. The Suez Canal was opened in 1869, and Cairo received a face-lift, complete with luxury hotels and an opera house, which was opened with Verdi's *Aida*. By the 1890s, Egypt had become as fashionable a resort as the Riviera, and in 1893 the Orient Express was carrying glamorous passengers between Paris and Istanbul. Painters Melling and Preziosi followed Liotard and Vanmour to Turkey: Lewis, Flaubert, de Nerval, Gérôme, and Florence Nightingale journeyed to Egypt; Delacroix to Algeria. Although he would never set foot inside a harem, Eugène Delacroix claimed that a man actually allowed him to peek into one. The result was the exquisite *Women of Algiers in Their Room*, which he painted in 1834. Ten years later he painted another version of the same scene.

John Frederick Lewis

From 1841 until 1851, John Frederick Lewis, a talented dandy from London, was a resident of Cairo. Wearing a turban, a glittering scimitar dangling at his side, he rode through the streets on a gray horse. He adopted the posture of a languid lotus eater and lived what William Makepeace Thackeray described as the "dreamy, hazy, lazy, tobaccofied life" of a wealthy Moslem. Lewis made real the Orientalist's ultimate dream of changing costume and address, and assuming a separate identity. At first, it was a romantic game, but gradually it consumed him, prompting beautiful canvases authentically portraying life behind the shutters.

Lewis avoided the tourist attractions most other Europeans sought and mingled instead with the people of Cairo. He worked restlessly, painting harems, bazaars, and street scenes as they truly were, without moralizing.

In his *Notes From a Journey* (1844), Thackeray describes visiting Lewis in Cairo. Thackeray was escorted into the salon of a Mameluke-style man-

sion, with a carved, gilt ceiling, decorated with arabesques and prime samples of calligraphy. From the courtyard, he noticed two enormous, flirtatious black eyes peering through the lattices. Lewis pretended it was only the cook, but Thackeray was convinced she had to be *la belle esclave*. After all, every man was entitled to at least one odalisque.

The Romantics

Lord Byron considered himself a great Oriental traveler, but, for him, the Orient was limited to Constantinople, the Bosphorus, and the Hellespont. The romantic works of Byron, Coleridge, Victor Hugo, Gustave Flaubert, and Théophile Gautier stood in exotic contrast to the grimy rationality of the industrial revolution sweeping Europe. Victor Hugo's *Les Orientales,* in its passionate depiction of captive souls, inspired canvases; Montesquieu's *Persian Letters* prompted Lecomte du Nouy's sensuous painting *Koshru's Dream*.

Gérard de Nerval traveled through the Orient carrying two Arabic words, *tayeb* (assent) and *mafish* (rejection). In his *Voyage en Orient* (1843–51), he laid bare the emotions behind his own pursuit of a slave woman named Zetnaybia: "There is something extremely captivating and irresistible in a woman from a faraway country; her costumes and habits are already singular enough to strike you, she speaks an unknown language and has, in short, none of those vulgar shortcomings to which we have become only too accustomed among the women in our own country."

But after attaining the slave woman, de Nerval does not quite know how to integrate her into his life. What should he do with her now? In this wonderful encounter, we come face to face with a clash of cultures and are not certain who is the slave and who the master. Unsuccessful in civilizing Zetnaybia and unable to accept her "primitive" idiosyncracies, he frees her.

In 1849, Gustave Flaubert, with his friend Maxime du Camp, set off for the Orient, which had long haunted his imagination. Like de Nerval, Flaubert glorified the seductions of Oriental women. He spent a year in Egypt and kept a diary full of extremely erotic and sensuous detail: "Kuchuk shed her clothing as she danced. Finally she was naked except for a *fichu* which she held in her hands and behind which she pretended to hide, and at the end she threw down the *fichu*. That was the Bee. . . . Finally, after repeating for us the wonderful step she had danced in the afternoon, she sank down breathless on her divan, her body continuing to move slightly in rhythm." This leads to an incredible night of passion with the *alme* (dancer)

Kuchuk. Flaubert describes his experience in detail candid enough to have made his mistress, Louise Colet, extremely jealous. Many years later, the experience inspired *Salammbo,* a novel of ancient Carthage.

Oriental female dancers intrigued even the otherwise detached poet, Théophile Gautier:

> *They stir strange nostalgias, dredge up infinite memories and conjure forth previous existences that come straying back in random array. Moorish dancing consists in perpetual undulations of the body: twisting of the lower back, swaying of the hips, movements of the arms, hands waving handkerchiefs, languid facial expressions, eyelids fluttering, eyes flashing or swooning, nostrils quivering, lips parted, bosoms heaving, necks bent like the throats of love sick doves . . . all these explicitly betoken the mysterious drama of voluptuousness.*

Such scenes fascinated both men and women. On watching the gyrations of a dancer's breasts, Lady Duff Gordon opined, "They were just like pomegranates and gloriously independent of any support."

Jean-Léon Gérôme

Photographic companies such as Bonfils and Son had been active in the East since the 1860s. In 1888, Kodak brought out a portable camera any tourist could operate. By the end of the nineteenth century, photography and photographers such as Francis Frith had severely curtailed the growth of Orientalist painting. However, some painters, like Gérôme, who became one of the most influential voices on the nineteenth-century art scene, took advantage of the new invention, using it in the creation of their own paintings. In 1854, Gérôme, whose accuracy of detail no less a figure than Théophile Gautier praised, traveled to Turkey and, later, to Egypt, Palestine, Syria, Sinai, and North Africa. With the help of his sketches and photographs, he was able to recreate with remarkable accuracy daring color schemes and unsurpassed detail of scenes. Especially fascinated by the Turkish baths, he often went to hamams with his sketchbooks to capture background material: "Stark naked perched on a stool, my box of paints across my knees, my palette in one hand . . . I felt slightly grotesque."

Although Gérôme never did get inside harems, his paintings can easily be perceived as visual counterparts of Lady Montagu's or Julia Pardoe's descriptions of bath scenes and other aspects of harem life. Revealed through a mist of steam, his women are always perfect and otherworldly.

Gérôme's marriage to the daughter of the influential art dealer Adolphe Goupil helped disseminate reproductions of his work, which became popular throughout the world, bringing harem scenes not only to the wealthy but, it seemed, to every prosaic household as well.

Amadeo Count Preziosi

Unlike Gérôme's oils, Amadeo Preziosi's watercolors display a quality of immediacy and robust realism similar to Lewis's work, although, in other respects, they are quite different in style. A Maltese count, Preziosi was born of a privileged family. When his father opposed his art career, he moved to Constantinople, living there for almost half a century. He was quick to

Amadeo Count Preziosi, Adile Hanim, *1854, Watercolor and pencil on paper, 10⅝ x 9⅝ in., Victoria and Albert Museum, London*

become associated with the European diplomatic community and to develop a reputation within it. From the 1840s to the 1870s, he supplied images of the city's life for travelers to take home. He lived in Pera, the European part of the city, married a Greek woman, and had three daughters and a son, whose descendants still live in Turkey. During the last decade of his life, he became the court painter to Sultan Abdulhamid II.

A connoisseur, Preziosi selected images of extremely colorful and interesting individuals, yet all of his subjects are clearly flesh and blood, not stylized clichés from *One Thousand and One Nights*. The portrait of Adile Hanim, for example, shows a real person, somewhat exotic, but still exuding an emotional complexity that anyone can identify with. This approach was a radical attitude toward the East, which traditionally had been represented by one-dimensional harem girls, depicted in conformity with prevailing European notions of beauty.

Preziosi painted not a glorified version of the East but the prosaic vitality of its everyday life. An odalisque reclines on a bed of pillows in her harem apartment, women picnic at the Sweet Waters of Asia, a Nubian slave attends an odalisque who smokes a chibuk and drinks coffee, women finger silk at the bazaar, a widow and her child visit a cemetery, an old water carrier leers at a young girl who coyly draws her veil.

Empress Eugénie

On her way to Egypt, to celebrate the opening of the Suez Canal, Empress Eugénie, wife of Napoleon III, visited Istanbul. For the first time in history, a sultan bowed before a woman. In her honor, Abdulaziz built a palace in Beylerbey and decorated it in French rococo style with an Oriental accent. Eugénie slept in a Syrian bed, richly inlaid with mother-of-pearl, tortoise-shell, and silver, and she bathed in a sumptuous hamam. She visited the women in the sultan's harem.

This visit began a chain of irreversible effects. The Turkish women living in harems suddenly acquired a taste for everything French. *Franco-mania* in Turkey became the counterpart of *Turquomania* in France. Aristocratic Turkish ladies copied the empress's appearance to the best of their ability, dividing their hair in the middle and spending endless hours making clusters of curls. High-heeled shoes replaced the curved-toed Turkish slippers. Skirts were suddenly favored over the *shalwar* (harem pants). Women in harems began reading Flaubert and Loti. Before the end of the century, the sultanas were dressed by the French couture house of Worth.

*Franz Xavier
Winterhalter,*
Empress Eugénie,
*1855, Oil on canvas,
Musée d'Orsay, Paris*

Pierre Loti

On the other side of the Bosphorus from the Beylerbey Palace where the empress stayed, in the hills of Eyub, overlooking the Golden Horn, is an open-air café called Café Pierre Loti. Here the famous author once lived, under an assumed identity as a Turkish bey. On many weekends, I went there with my friends. We sat under the century-old sycamores, sipping black tea served in samovars and digesting the view. What we saw were shipyards, paper factories, and enormous mountains of coal—no longer a "city of cut jasper," featuring the romantic vista of Sweet Waters with myriad colorful kayiks. But we still fantasized that city, because Loti had evoked it so well for us in his novels.

Born into a Huguenot family as Julien Viaud, Loti joined the Navy as a young man, wanting to see the world. His voyages took him to the most exotic and far-off places; in each, Loti pursued rose-colored romance and wrote books about love affairs with beautiful women of strange cultures. Evocative and nostalgic, his novels speak of melancholy, disenchantment, incurable solitude, and death.

No place, however, enthralled him so much as Istanbul. It was love at first sight. He had found *his* subject and, with it, he formed a lifelong love affair, producing two gems of Orientalist literature, *Aziyade* (1877) and *The Disenchanted* (1906). Loti lived what he wrote: "Behind those heavy iron bars, two large eyes were fixed on me. The eyebrows were drawn across, so that they met. . . . A white veil was wound tightly around the head, leaving only the brow, and those great eyes free. They were green—that sea-green which poets of the Orient once sang." This was Aziyade, whose enigmatic and untouchable beauty consumed Loti. She was a Circassian kadin in the harem of a bey. Defying all danger, Loti's servant Samuel arranged a nocturnal rendezvous. They met on a boat:

> *Aziyade's barque is filled with soft rugs, cushions and Turkish coverlets—all the refinements and nonchalance of the Orient, so that it seems a floating bed, rather than a barque. . . . All dangers surround this bed of ours, which drifts slowly out to sea: it is as if two beings are united there to taste the intoxicating pleasure of the impossible.*
>
> *When we are far enough from all else, she holds out her arms to me. I reach her side, trembling as I touch her. At this first contact I am filled with mortal languor: her veils are impregnated with all the perfumes of the Orient, her flesh is firm and cool.*

The prose is purple, and the fantasy boundless. Loti and Aziyade have many such nights of pleasure on her boat. Finally, Loti's ship has to leave; the lovers part; he promises to return. But he does not, and Aziyade dies of a broken heart.

After Aziyade's death, heartbroken himself, Loti did not return to Istanbul for almost twenty years. In the meantime, it had become the West's turn to influence the East. Eastern women began learning foreign languages and attending schools; by the turn of the century, though they still lived in harems, they were a new breed, well-educated and outspoken, envious of European women's freedom, longing to shed their veils, show their faces, and even choose their own husbands.

Loti received a letter from such a woman, named Djénane, who entreated him to come to Istanbul. Beginning to age, tempted to see Aziyade's land once again, he decided to return. This was the beginning of a novel called *The Disenchanted*.

Djénane and two accomplices arranged clandestine meetings with Loti in the most exotic and romantic parts of Istanbul. The women filled him with heartbreaking accounts of their miserable lives, in the hope of persuading Loti to write a novel about the suffering of women still living in harems.

Photograph of a 1905 drawing by Auguste Rodin, which depicts the heroines of Pierre Loti's harem novel, The Disenchanted. *Collection of the author*

Henri Rousseau,
Pierre Loti,
ca. 1910, Oil on
canvas, 24 x 19⅝ in.,
Kunsthaus Zürich

The novelist was less interested in politics than in romance, so the women fabricated a tale straight out of *One Thousand and One Nights.* What they had failed to anticipate was his falling in love with Djénane, and how such an affair would place all of their lives in peril. To make Loti leave Istanbul, they staged a fake funeral, pretending Djénane, like Aziyade, had died of a heart broken by forbidden love.

Loti returned to Paris and wrote *The Disenchanted* (1906).

But the story does not end here. Soon after the writer's departure, the women on whom the book was based also fled to Paris, where they became a *cause célèbre,* appearing at the most exclusive parties. They were written about, painted, and sculpted by the greatest artists of the era, among them Henri Rousseau and Auguste Rodin. Moreover, after Loti's death, a French woman named Madame Lera, who wrote under the pseudonym Marc Helys, published *Le Secret des désenchantées,* which purported to reveal that she herself had posed as Djénane with the help of her two Turkish friends;

the three women had simply wanted to amuse themselves with Loti. Marc Helys's "revelation" was challenged, but no one knows for sure whether she was writing fiction or reporting fact.

Emancipation of the East

The publication of *The Disenchanted* not only stirred up scandal, it brought the suffragettes to the rescue. Turkey was suddenly flooded with European women who were appalled at the situation of their sisters, still living under such submission. They set out on a crusade to free these unfortunates. Eastern women had always held an interest for European feminists. Sir Richard Burton's wife, Isabelle, would deliberately appear in low-cut dresses during social gatherings to set a provocative example, and in Lebanon, at an embassy reception, she had the wives sit in chairs and ordered their husbands to serve them tea and cakes.

In Turkey, the inevitable uprising of women was under way by the turn of the century. The social upheaval so threatened the established order that in 1901 Sultan Abdul Hamid II issued an edict prohibiting the employment of Christian teachers in harems, the education of Turkish children in foreign schools, and the appearance in public of Turkish women with foreign women. These restrictions only served to force the issue among women, who rebelled by secretly meeting and organizing. Messages were carried from harem to harem—protected by the certainty that Moslem women are never searched. The "Young Turks," idealistic poets and intellectuals, expressed their own feelings of shame about perpetuating polygamy. Faced with the stark reality of a diseased empire, they shed their intellectual idealism and began mobilizing in Macedonia. In 1909, they overthrew the sultan and established a constitutional government. It would take another decade for major changes actually to become effective in Turkish society, but by the 1920s women became fully integrated into public life. The revolutionary leader Kemal Atatürk challenged: "Is it possible that, while one half of a community stays chained to the ground, the other half can rise to the skies? There is no question—the steps of progress must be taken to accomplish the various stages of the journey into the land of progress and renovation. If this is done, our revolution will be successful."

Veils came off. The massive layers of clothing were shed and, with them, the years of suppression and isolation. Harems were declared unlawful; polygamy abolished.

My maternal grandfather, Hamdi Bey, a "Young Turk," ca. 1908

The Last Picture

One of the most touching and strange scenes took place at the Seraglio. Relatives of the harem women were summoned to Istanbul to claim their daughters and sisters. Circassian mountaineers and peasants came in droves, clad in the picturesque costume of country folk. They were formally ushered into a large hall of the Seraglio where the ex-Sultan's kadins, concubines, and odalisques came to greet them. The contrast between the elegantly dressed ladies of the palace and the rugged peasant men was dramatic. Everywhere people fell into the arms of their long-unseen loved ones, sobbing uncontrollably. But the most heartbreaking picture was the faces of the women for whom no one came. Kismet left them to the hollow echoes of a dead institution, which, even in their freedom, they could not escape. They remained at the Old Palace, relics of the past, trapped in their own liberation. Artists continued immortalizing these beauties with stories of perfumed handkerchiefs, roses, and poems dropped from behind latticed windows.

Survivals

Twentieth-Century Orientalism

Meanwhile, in the West, the passion for the Orient was rekindled with a new translation of the *One Thousand and One Nights* (1899–1904) by Dr. Joseph-Charles Mardrus. Once again, Orientalism was fashionable, the enthusiasm for it continuing well into the thirties, inspiring dance, opera, and fashion, as well as painting and the magical new medium, movies. Even circuses and vaudeville troups used the splendors of the Orient in their own evocations.

Sergei Diaghilev's Ballets Russes, performing in Paris in 1910, was undeniably one of the most spectacular sources of the West's reinfection by the Orient. Cecil Beaton recalls the titillation of watching Karsavina dance with Nijinsky, dressed as the golden slave, making superhuman leaps in *Scheherazade*. The spectacular sets and costumes for the Parisian presentation were designed in wild, orgiastic colors by the Russian painter Leon Bakst. The plot of Diaghilev's *Scheherazade* is audacious. Harem women, taking advantage of the sultan's absence, indulge in an orgy with the eunuchs. Gore and blood abound when the sultan unexpectedly returns.

A year later, the famous couturier Paul Poiret presented Paris society with a new harem look. Fabrics like Damascus silk, crêpe de Chine, crêpe de Maroc, and Ottoman and Smyrna brocade woven in rich, exotic colors replaced the soft, pale pastels of the preceding era. Poiret was a cunning promoter. In order to introduce his new line of couture, he threw an extravagant Persian Ball, the "Mille et deuxième nuit." Dressed as a sultan, the rotund designer received hundreds of guests amid exotic birds and monkeys, bare-breasted black women, Oriental rugs, and copper braziers in which attar of roses and sandalwood smoldered. During the next few seasons, Oriental parties became the craze.

Later, Poiret started an interior-design company to provide the appropriate decor for his harem fashions. Parisian salons were converted into colorful harems with rich draperies, Oriental rugs, and heaps of cushions. Poiret also launched a line of perfumes called Rosine, with names like Minaret, Nuit de Chine, Antinea, and Aladdin.

By the late teens, innumerable women were dressing themselves as favorites of the harem, still imagining that in the East women lived exquisite

Leon Bakst, Costume design for Le Pélerin, *1912, The Fine Art Society, London*

193

lives of sensual abandon. Liane de Pougy describes women lunching at the Lido in 1926, looking "as though they were acting in a fairy tale: Scheherazade, Salome, Salammbo—Oriental ladies from rich harems—sumptuous pajamas, brilliantly-colored and glittering."

"Women acted as if they were odalisques trying to fascinate a Pasha, instead of respectable matrons tied up to British gentlemen whose minds were entirely fixed on guns, dogs and birds," mused the Duchess of Westminster.

The Colonial Exhibitions in Marseilles in 1922 introduced another exotic marketing strategy. Posters with harem beauties advertised face creams, cosmetics, and scents with names like Jerusalem, Ambre de Nubie, or Secret de Sphinx. Packagers made use of the same voluptuaries to sell Turkish cigarettes with names like Murad and Sobranie. Merchants had discovered the enormous marketing power of Oriental sensuality. This obsession continues to our day. We still use perfumes named Opium, Naima, Shalimar, Damascus. Haute couture still drapes on Western bodies lush fabrics that originated on the Silk Road. Designers like Yves Saint-Laurent, Rifat Ozbek, and Oscar de la Renta continue to be inspired by harem pants, fezes, embroidered vests, and elegant bustiers.

During the first three decades of the twentieth century, the French in Algeria, obsessed by Algerian women, circulated postcards all over the

Left:
A harem beauty promoting Murad Turkish cigarettes

Right:
The image of the Grand Odalisque used to promote ESB Speakers (November 1987; Mark Hess, illustrator; Wynn Medinger, designer)

world, creating a fantasy, much as the Orientalist paintings of the previous century had, simply by including in the composition a few props, such as nargilehs, chibuks, coffee accoutrements, the backdrop of an Oriental carpet, and a girl.

Despite the advent of photography and abstract art, the odalisque was still a fine excuse for depicting the female figure in exotic environments. Throughout the twenties, Henri Matisse painted the most fabulous series of odalisques. As with the earliest Orientalists, his artistic harem deviated from actuality. "Look closely at the Odalisques: the sun floods them with its triumphant brightness, taking hold of colors and forms. Now the Oriental decor of the interiors, the array of hangings and rugs, the rich costumes, the

Matisse drawing from a model in his apartment on Place Charles Félix, Nice, ca. 1928, Photograph courtesy the Museum of Modern Art, New York

*Henri Matisse,
Odalisque with
Magnolias, 1923,
Oil on canvas,
23³/₄ x 32 in.,
Private collection*

*Henri Matisse,
Odalisque with Red
Trousers, 1922,
Oil on canvas,
26³/₈ x 33 in.,
Musée National d'Art
Moderne, Centre
Georges Pompidou,
Paris*

sensuality of heavy, drowsy bodies, the blissful torpor in the eyes lying in wait for pleasure, all this splendid display of siesta elevated to the maximum intensity of arabesque and color should not delude us," Matisse suggested.

Scenes from Ali Baba Goes to Town, *1937, starring Eddie Cantor*

Movies and Television

Meanwhile, a new visual and commercial art, film, was capitalizing on the public's perpetual fascination with images Oriental. Now harem beauties could be seen actually shaking their hips and rattling their breasts. Handsome sheiks ravaged these odalisques, reinforcing the myth of women's need to be possessed. Throughout the twenties, Rudolph Valentino prospered on

the Western world's eternal need for escape. As journalist Anne Edwards commented: "When a sheik with passion burning in his eyes gallops up just as you are about to be forced to give your troth to one you don't love, and sweeps you into a saddle and away to love in a tent in the desert—that's film stuff, my child."

Istanbul Express, Mask of Demitrios, Ali Baba and the Forty Thieves, Ali

Baba Goes to Town, Thief of Bagdad, Kismet, and numerous other films continued into the sound era, glorifying the romance of the East. In the sixties and seventies, television matched an all-American boy (in a U.S. Air Force uniform) with an all-American girl (in diaphanous Oriental costume) in "I Dream of Jeannie." Fellini's *Amarcord* (1973) portrayed an outrageously flamboyant harem; and James Bond thrillers habitually surrounded 007 with a bevy of pretty, sparsely clad women. Recently, *The Witches of Eastwick* (1984), John Updike's novel (also made into a film), recreated the harem fantasy in a gothic American setting.

Harems Today

As harems slowly dissolved out of the Eastern consciousness, they carved their niche in the West's. One of the most frequent questions people ask is, "Do harems still exist?"

They do.

Polygamy has been outlawed in Turkey and China, the two greatest harem nations, but is still a flourishing practice in the Middle East and Africa. In India, for example, having multiple wives is illegal but common nonetheless. Concubines are an accepted part of a man's life. A wife is traditionally the mother of children and keeper of the house, whereas a concubine is exclusively for sexual pleasure. In Saudi Arabia, "rivals" still live in the same house and are veiled when they leave—in Cadillacs rather than carriages. Eighty-seven percent of traditional African societies still practice polygamy. In Nigeria, men are allowed to take four wives. In 1952, the *fon* (chief of a settlement) was reputed to have six hundred wives. (In actuality, he had only a hundred or so.)

Harems linger as part of the polygamous Islamic tradition, and they are perhaps being reinforced by the "fundamentalist" wave that has swept through Iran and is reputedly spreading to other Moslem countries. But what is even more astonishing is that harems exist in the *Western* world—although we may not always think of them as such.

The Church of Jesus Christ of Latter-Day Saints established polygamy in 1831. For many years the Mormons practiced "plural marriage" secretly, since it was (and is) illegal in the United States. In 1890 the Church declared against polygamy; devout fundamentalists have continued practicing it underground.

In her insightful memoir, *In My Father's House* (1984), Dorothy Allred Solomon chronicles growing up in her Mormon father's harem with seven

mothers and forty-eight brothers and sisters. In this household, a strong hierarchy existed, based on seniority among the women, and not all the wives were happy with their positions in the pecking order. Eventually, the threat of arrest forced Solomon's father to set up separate homes for his wives and visit each secretly.

In certain spiritual communes, especially among those practicing Eastern religions that sanction polygamy, harems still flourish. Some of the
gurus exercise as much autonomy as a sultan. Bhagwan Shree Rajneesh and
Bubba Free John, for example, had concubines. More commercial enter-
prises include Hugh Hefner's Playboy mansion, where live-in "bunnies"
abound to fulfill the master's wishes. In novels and films, James Bond has
represented the male fantasy of possessing a multitude of beautiful and ador-
ing women. And, on the seamier side, the pornography market is flooded
with bondage magazines and paraphernalia, which in essence are versions of
the slave-master rituals. There is, finally, no better way to sell a product
than to show a man surrounded and adored by sexy women. In these ways,
then, concubines and harems still exist as part of the matrix of contemporary
Western society. Sociologist Joseph Scott believes that polygamous relationships are the best-kept secrets in America; 5 percent of the American population is estimated actually to practice some form of polygamy.

We have not answered some of the fundamental questions, such as whether
men are by nature polygamous. There is every indication that we act as if
we believe this to be the case—until marriage, at which point we expect
polygamous longings to dematerialize. The idea of a harem mythologizes
whatever polygamous longings men entertain. I have not yet met a man
who fails to be titillated by the harem fantasy.

And women: are they by nature polyandrous? If so, why do we have
so few examples of this practice, historical or otherwise? Is it because the age
of patriarchy has subjugated this natural impulse? The matriarchal era, preceding the ascent of Judeo-Christian religions, saw instances of powerful
queens and priestesses—Semiramis, Ishtar, Cleopatra—having several men.
Female archetypes such as "la belle dame sans merci," who bewitch, seduce,
and destroy innocent males, occur in early mythology and have evolved into
such pop figures as the vamp, femme fatale, and black widow. However,
all these phantasms involve serial, rather than simultaneous, possession of
mates. Polyandry does not seem to have become institutionalized in the
manner of the harems.

There is no doubt that the image of an odalisque occupies a significant
part in the feminine unconscious. Through interviews, during which I asked
women to list the most appealing female roles they would like to play in a
movie, I discovered that an odalisque—the image of total submission, stupor, and surrender—was among the most common. Nevertheless, not
many of the women had a fantasy of being an inmate of a harem, and few

admitted to a desire for such servitude and anonymity. For the majority, the word *harem* evoked a different response; a sadness came over women's eyes as they talked. I could sense that the pain of loss and jealousy was clouding their vision. Many, however, seemed to sway toward communalism, a tribal yearning to be with other women. No, not to share a lover. But to be together.

Audrey B. Chapman, in *Man Sharing* (1986), relates interviews with two American women who have quietly chosen polygamy. One, Delores, expressed her general insecurity about the traditional American marriage. She entered into a polygamous marriage because she believed polygamy created a more stable family life. Delores felt safe knowing at all times where her husband was: "He is either at work or with one of the wives whom I know very well. As head wife, I helped him select these other women, and we get along very well most of the time. I never feel the rejection I did in my first marriage, because we have a system where each wife has a specified time with our husband. We are all involved in scheduling the calendar with our husband, so no one feels threatened by any rivalry." What is unusual is that, in this harem, women have a voice and are not mere slaves.

In another interview, we learn that Karen chose a polygamous marriage because she was tired of struggling with "all the feelings of ownership and possession. I don't see my husband as a possession. We are a family unit and we make decisions that are best for everyone, and I like this." Further discussion with Karen revealed that she and her co-wife did not compare notes concerning sex. Each had separate bedrooms, which the husband never entered. Instead, they visited him in his room—though this did not occur frequently, since their spiritual connection was much more important than their physical one. Again, unlike the women in a traditional harem, Karen exercised choice. Also, both women expressed their feelings of a strong sense of sisterhood with the other co-wives. Instead of rivalry, they shared support and understanding.

I once saw an enormous outdoor tub surrounded by an oak grove. A dozen or so women were submerged in the water, rose petals floating on its surface. The women passed around tall glasses of cold fruit juices. Silence predominated, interrupted only occasionally by a wave of laughter and chatter, murmuring, female murmuring, which suddenly died into utter silence. The women, with their breathing, were yielding to the hum of nature. Wet, tangled hair. Flushed cheeks. (A friend who takes erotic photographs of women once told me that she has her subjects take a hot bath first, so that

the steam brings on a flushed appearance, adding mystery and desire to the face.) They climbed in and out of the tub, vapor forming clouds around their bodies, bodies of all kinds, fat and flabby, lean and taut, young and old. Then they regrouped in poses of abandon—kneeling, reclining, sitting cross-legged. They seemed comfortable touching each other, massaging the kinks, rubbing in botanicals and sweet-smelling salts and oils. I watched them cover their faces with clay, their bodies with cornmeal and avocado, their hair with henna. They were plastering a mixture of lemon and caramel on their legs, and crying out as they pulled it off. They seemed utterly at ease, being together and knowing how to take care of one another.

This is not the re-creation of a scene from an Orientalist painting. Nor are the women Sapphic. I am recalling a contemporary women's retreat. The signs and rituals utter a shared consciousness that supersedes history or social institutions.

Pablo Picasso, Women of Algiers I, 1955, Oil on canvas, 38¼ x 51 in., Norton Simon Art Foundation, Pasadena, California

When women gather, I observe that something almost archetypal happens: overflowing and abundance, complicity and lack of censorship, lack of the posturing that inevitably dominates a mixed group. Primitive rituals evolve. The women synchronize with the moon's phases. They have an instinct for the earth, the water, an affinity for the timeless activities of bathing and grooming, for growing things.

And men? This is not what happens when tribes of men come together. This is not the way men choose to act with one another. They seem to miss the closeness, the texture of the women's world, a world they enter only through association with women. In this view, the harem is a re-creation of a nostalgic need, a return to childhood and to mothers. For a man, it is an attempt to own a world of his own, utterly egocentric, without the intrusion of other men. No wonder *valide*—or mother—was the axis of the harem.

The roots of slavery and isolation are in the womb. And the womb, like the harem, is sacrosanct.

An adult male is not encouraged to admit to the desire for the womb, a state of isolated suspension. *Real men don't*. He has gained consciousness, tasted food, sex, and death.

Nevertheless, he yearns to return to the womb, bringing with him all his worldly acquisitions—his very own womb, protected by his mother, within her, his desires shielded from territoriality; his own world, where no other male can enter—except his sons, of course, and even those he admits reluctantly. To guard his place, he creates servants who have been neutralized. He brings his wife and all the other women he desires—perhaps all reflections of the Great Mother.

This he calls paradise.

Is polygamy—harem—less acceptable than a monogamous system in which such desires and inclinations are just as intense but privately experienced, in which one has the same hates and jealousies, endures the same struggle for survival, feels the same fear of open vulnerability, undertakes, too, the same search for sisterhood and union, oneness with other beings? After all, the Mormon system of "sealing" women with their husbands— that is, uniting their souls after death—was an acknowledgment of togetherness not only in this life but through eternity. Husband and wife are parts of the same soul, yearning to become One. (It seems, though, that some Mormons became excessively ambitious: "At the turn of the century when Mormons were still practicing polygamy, some church officials had themselves sealed [at the Morman archives in Utah] with such famous women as Cleopatra and Queen Elizabeth with the idea that after death, they would be able to claim these women as their wives," according to Rachel Wrege in a 1982 article.)

We cannot look at history and expect our contemporary perceptions to apply. His-story is a male sport, the story of men, as told by men through the ages. Women figure in it simply to patch the silent phrases. But there is an uncanny resemblance between rituals of forgotten history and the reign of the feminine unconscious.

Harem cannot be explained simply through the mirror of history. Harem is a unique archetype of the collective unconscious—matriarchy incubating in the cradle of patriarchy. It is an unsolved enigma, a haunting mystery, and undeniably an incredible source of intuitive intelligence. It is a shadow world—full of halftones, large areas obscured or lost forever— which we are reluctant to own as our own creation. It belongs in the realm of dark secrets and fears we prefer not to remember. It is about forgetfulness.

It requires returning to our subjective experience and splicing it together with imagination and intuition, to open the "sesame" of the one thousand and one chambers of our dreams.

For me, it started at the Topkapi Palace, with a walk through the Grand Harem, now a museum—a graveyard of the past, barren and colorless, stripped of fantasies. But the walls seemed to whisper. The walls seemed to whisper.

In the baths, the boudoirs, the courtyards of the harem women, we start with a tabula rasa—or, rather, with a mysterious text written in invisible ink. The walls whisper, the intricate labyrinths flow into blood memories. The veil is still drawn, but it is diaphanous, in my mind now. A provocative assemblage.

Chronology

Bibliography

Acknowl-
edgments

Index

Chronology of the Ottoman Sultans

Sultans		Sultanas	
1. Osman I	(1299–1326)		
2. Orhan	(1326–60)	Theodora	
3. Murad I	(1360–89)		
4. Beyazid I	(1389–1402)		
Interregnum			
5. Mehmed I	(1431–21)		
6. Murad II	(1421–40; 1445–51)		
7. Mehmed II	(1440–45; 1451–81)	Irene	
8. Beyazid II	(1481–1512)		
9. Selim I	(1520–66)		
10. Süleyman I	(1520–66)	Roxalena	
11. Selim II	(1566–74)		
12. Murad III	(1574–95)	Baffa	
13. Mehmed III	(1595–1603)		
14. Ahmed I	(1603–17)	Kösem	The Reign of Women (1541–1687)
15. Mustafa I	(1617; 1622–23)		
16. Osman II	(1617–22; 1622–23)		
17. Murad IV	(1623–40)		
18. Ibrahim	(1640–48)	Turhan	

Sultans		Sultanas
19. Mehmed IV	(1648–87)	
20. Süleyman II	(1687–91)	
21. Ahmed II	(1691–95)	
22. Mustafa II	(1695–1703)	
23. Ahmed III	(1703–30)	
24. Mahmud I	(1730–54)	
25. Osman III	(1754–57)	
26. Mustafa III	(1757–74)	
27. Abdülhamid I	(1774–89)	Aimée de Rivery
28. Selim III	(1789–1807)	
29. Mustafa IV	(1807–8)	
30. Mahmud II	(1808–39)	
31. Abdülmecid	(1839–61)	
32. Abdülaziz	(1861–76)	
33. Murad V	(1876)	
34. Abdülhamid II	(1876–1909)	
35. Mehmed V	(1909–18)	
36. Mehmed VI	(1918–22)	

Bibliography

Alderson, A. D. *Structure of the Ottoman Dynasty*. Oxford, 1956.

Alexandre, Arsene, ed. *The Decorative Art of Leon Bakst*. London, 1913.

Alireza, Marianne. *At the Drop of a Veil*. Boston, 1971.

Alloula, Malek. *The Colonial Harem*. Minneapolis, 1986.

Amicis, Edmondo de. *Constantinople*. 2 vols. Philadelphia, 1896.

Angiolello, Gio Maria. *Historia Turchesa*. 1480.

Arzik, Nimet. *Osmanli Saraylarinda Yabanci Kadin Sultanlar*. Istanbul, 1969.

Bassano da Zara, Luigi. *I Costumi et i modi particolari de la vita de Turchi*. Rome, 1545.

Beckford, William. *Vathek*. London, 1786.

Behr, Edward. *The Last Emperor*. New York, 1987.

Birsel, Salah. *Boğaziçi Şingir Mingir*. Ankara, 1981.

Blanch, Lesley. *Pierre Loti*. New York, 1983.

———. *The Wilder Shores of Love*. New York, 1954.

Blunt, Lady Anne. *Bedouin Tribes of the Euphrates*. London, 1919.

———. *A Pilgrimage to Nejd*. London, 1881.

Bon, Ottaviano. *Seraglio of the Grand Signor (1608)*. Venice, 1865.

Bowles, Paul. *The Sheltering Sky*. New York, 1949.

Burckhardt, J. T. *Travels in Arabia*. London, 1822.

Burton, Isabel. *The Life of Captain Sir Richard F. Burton*. London, 1893.

Burton, Sir Richard F. *Personal Narrative of a Pilgrimage to Al-Madinah and Meccah*. London, 1853.

———. *The Thousand Nights and a Night*. London, 1887.

Busbecq, Ogier Ghiselin de. *Life and Letters*. 2 vols. London, 1881.

Celal, Musahipzade. *Eski Istanbul Yaşayişi*. Istanbul, 1946.

Chapman, Audrey B. *Man Sharing*. New York, 1986.

Chelebi, Evliya. *Seyahatname*. Istanbul, 1834.

Chelebi, Sinan. *Saadabad*. Istanbul, 1750.

Chelkowski, Peter J. *Mirror of the Invisible World*. New York, 1975.

Cowart, Jack, and Dominique Fourcade. *Henri Matisse: The Early Years in Nice (1916–1930)*. Washington, D.C., 1986.

Dallam, Thomas. *Early Voyages and Travels in the Levant*. London, 1893.

Davey, Richard. *The Sultan and His Subjects*. 2 vols. New York, 1897.

Davis, Raphaela. *Everyday Life in Ottoman Turkey*. London, 1971.

Dinet, Etienne. *Tableaux de la vie Arabe.* Paris, 1908.

Du Camp, Maxime. *Souvenirs et paysages d'Orient.* Paris, 1849.

Duff Gordon, Lady Lucie. *Letters from Egypt.* London, 1865.

Durukan, Zeynep M. *The Harem of Topkapi Palace.* Istanbul, 1973.

Ellison, Grace. *Turkey Today.* London, 1928.

El Saadawi, Nawal. *The Hidden Face of Eve.* Boston, 1980.

Enderuni, Fazil. *Hübanname-Zenanname.* Istanbul, 1793.

Esin, Emel. *Turkish Miniature Painting.* New York, 1960.

Ettinghausen, Richard, and Marie Lukens Swietochowski. *Islamic Painting.* New York, 1978.

Fernea, Elizabeth Warnock. *Guests of the Sheik.* New York, 1965.

Fitzgerald, Edward. *Rubaiyat of Omar Khayyam.* London, 1879.

Flachat, Jean-Claude. *Observations sur le commerce et sur les arts de l'Europe, de l'Asie, de l'Afrique, et même des Indes orientales.* Lyons, 1746.

Forster, Charles Thornton, and F. H. Blackburn Danniell. *The Life and Letters of Ogier Ghiselen de Busbecq.* 2 vols. London, 1881.

Fromentin, Eugene. *Une Année dans le Sahel, 1853.* Paris, 1912.

Galland, Antoine. *Journal pendant son sejour à Constantinople (1672–1673).* Paris, 1881.

Gautier, Theophile. *Constantinople.* Paris, 1854.

Gibbon, Edward. *The History of the Decline and Fall of the Roman Empire (1776–88)* Ed. J. B. Bury. 7 vols. London, 1896–1900.

Gibbons, Herbert Adams. *The Foundation of the Ottoman Empire.* Oxford, 1916.

Harding, James. *Artistes Pompiers.* London, 1972.

Harvey, Mrs. *Turkish Harems and Circassian Homes.* London, 1871.

Jacobs, Joseph. *Tulips.* New York, 1912.

Jenkins, Hester Donaldson. *Behind Turkish Lattices.* London, 1911.

Julian, Phillippe. *Orientalist.* Oxford, 1977.

Kinross, Lord. *The Ottoman Centuries.* London, New York, 1977.

Klunzinger, C. B. *Upper Egypt. Its People and Its Products.* London, 1878.

Knipp, Christopher. "Types of Orientalism in Eighteenth-Century England." Ph.D diss., University of California, Berkeley, 1974.

Koçu, Reşad Ekrem. *Topkapu Sarayi.* Istanbul, 1960.

Koseoğlu, Cengiz. *Harem.* Istanbul, 1979.

Kritzeck, James. *Anthology of Islamic Literature.* New York, 1966.

Lang, Andrew, ed. *The Arabian Nights Entertainments.* London, 1898.

Lear, Edward. *Journals.* London, 1952.

Levy, Michael. *The World of Ottoman Art.* New York, 1975.

Lewis, John Frederick. *Illustrations of Constantinople*. London, 1835–36.

Lewis, Raphaela. *Everyday Life in Ottoman Turkey*. London, New York, 1971.

Llewellyn, Briony. "Eastern Light." *FMR*, August 1984.

Llewellyn, Briony, and Charles Newton, eds. *The People and Places of Constantinople*. Watercolors by Amadeo Count Preziosi, 1816–1882. London, 1985.

Loti, Pierre. *Aziyade*. Paris, 1877.

———. *The Disenchanted*. New York, 1906.

Maupassant, Guy de. *Un Cas de divorce*. Paris, 1886.

Mehta, Rama. *Inside the Haveli*. Calcutta, 1977.

Melling, Antoine Ignaz. *Voyage pittoresque de Constantinople*. Paris, 1807–24.

Mikes, M. *Turkiye Mektuplari*. Ankara, 1944–45.

Miller, Barnette. *Beyond the Sublime Port*. New Haven, 1931.

Montagu, Lady Mary Wortley. *The Complete Letters*. London, 1708–1720.

Morton, Benjamin A. *The Veiled Empress*. New York, 1923.

Nerval, Gerard de. *Journey to the Orient*. New York, 1972.

Newton, Charles. "People of Constantinople." *FMR*, May 1985.

Nicolai, Nicolo di. *Le Navigationi et Viaggi, Fatti Nella Turchia*. Venice, 1580.

Nightingale, Florence. *Letters from Egypt, (1849–1850)*. New York, 1987.

d'Ohsson, Mouradja. *Tableau general de l'empire Ottoman*. Paris, 1788–1824.

Pardoe, Julia. *Beauties of the Bosphorus*. London, 1840.

———. *City of the Sultan*. London, 1837.

Pears, Edwin. *Forty Years in Constantinople*. London, 1916.

Penzer, N. M. *The Harem*. London, 1936.

Rasim, Ahmed. *Resimli ve Haritali Osmanli Tarihi*. Istanbul, 1910.

Refik, Ahmet. *Kadinlar Saltanati*. Istanbul, 1923.

———. *Kizlar Ağasi*. Istanbul, 1926.

Richards, John. *Diary on a Journey*. London, 1700.

Rosedale, H. G. *Queen Elizabeth and the Levant Company*. London, 1904.

Rycaut, Sir Paul. *History of the Ottoman Empire from the Year 1623 to 1677*. London, 1680.

Said, Edward W. *Orientalism*. New York, 1978.

Saz, Leyla. *Harem'in Içyüzü*. Istanbul, 1974.

Searight, Sarah. *The British in the Middle East*. London, 1969.

Seydi, Ali Bey. *Teşrifat ve Teşkilatimiz*. Istanbul, 1921.

Shaarawi, Huda. *Harem Years*. New York, 1986.

Sherwood, Shirley. *Venice Simplon Orient Express*. London, 1985.

Siyavuşgil, Sadri Esat. *Karagöz*. Istanbul, 1954.

Solomon, Dorothy Allred. *In My Father's House.* New York, 1984.

Steegmuller, Francis. *Flaubert in Egypt: Sensibility on Tour.* New York, 1972.

Taşkiran, Tezer. *Women in Turkey.* Istanbul, 1976.

Thackeray, William Makepeace. *Notes of a Journey.* London, 1844.

Thevenot, Jean. *1655–1656 da Turkiye.* Istanbul, 1978.

Thornton, Lynne. *Women as Portrayed in Orientalist Painting.* Paris, 1985.

Tuğlaci, Pars. *Osmanli Saray Kadinlari.* Istanbul, 1985.

Uluçay, Cağatay. *Harem.* Ankara, 1971.

———. *Harem'den Mektuplar.* Istanbul, 1956.

Unuvar, Safiye. *Saray Hatiralarim.* Istanbul, 1964.

Uşakligil, Halit Ziya. *Saray ve Ötesi.* 3 vols. Istanbul, 1940–42.

Vaka, Demetra. *Haremlik.* Boston, 1909.

Van-Lennep, H. J. *The Oriental Album.* New York, 1862.

Verrier, Michelle. *The Orientalists.* London, 1979.

Walsh, Robert. *Narrative of a Journey from Constantinople to England.* London, 1828.

Watney, John. *Travels In Araby of Lady Hester Stanhope.* London, 1975.

White, Charles. *Three Years in Constantinople.* London, 1846.

White, Palmer. *Paul Poiret.* London, 1973.

Acknowledgments

This book was a labor of love. Many people extended time, care, and generosity beyond belief. My father, Sadri, obsessively kept archives and precious family photographs. My mother, Yümniye, ingeniously excavated many of the original sources. Zehra and Meryem, women ancestors, made the world of harems very personal.

At Abbeville Press, gifted people walked me through each step of bookmaking with special care. Thank you, Lisa Peyton, Amy Handy, Mark Magowan, Steven Pincus, Sharon Gallagher, Alexandra Chapman, Hope Koturo, Deborah Sloan, and Carol Volk. Renée Khatami, the book's designer, created an inspired work of art. Alan Axelrod is a splendid editor who deserves a medal for his persistence. And Bob Abrams, my publisher, is a brilliant man with fine taste and intuition who made the book worthwhile.

Special thanks to Warren Cook, my agent and one of the finest men I know. Many thanks also to Carol Tarlow, Suzanne Lipsett, Carol Costello, Katherine Martin, Jeanine Kagan, Christine Stockton, Barbara Dills, the John Simon Guggenheim Foundation, Stephen Huyler, Christopher Knipp, George Csicsery, David Wakely, Carol Pitts, Morgan Barnes, Cynthia Jurs Hotchkiss, and Sandra Wilson. I've been lucky with people.

Finally: thank you, Robert Croutier, husband and best friend, for keeping the fire burning while I wrote.

Alev Lytle Croutier

Isma'il Jala'ir,
Ladies round a
samovar, *detail.*
See p. 99

Index

Page numbers in italics refer to illustrations.

Picture Credits

The photographers and sources of photographic material other than those indicated in the captions are as follows: Aurora Art Publishers, Leningrad: pages 34, 35; The Bettmann Archive, New York: dedication page, page 99; Peter and Georgina Bowater/The Image Bank: page 28;

Bridgeman Art Library, London: pages 133, 165 (bottom), 192; Culver Pictures, New York: pages 74, 75, 82 (top), 94, 166 (bottom); The Fine Art Society, London: pages 22, 31 (bottom), 102, 121; Kyburg Limited, London: page 65 (top); Portal Publications, Corte Madera, California: page 195 (left);

© Jake Rajs, New York/ The Image Bank: page 58 (top); Réunion des Musées Nationaux, Paris: pages 72, 164, 176, 180, 186; Roger-Viollet, Paris: page 141; The University of Minnesota Press, Minneapolis (reprinted from *The Colonial Harem* by Malek Alloula): page 154.

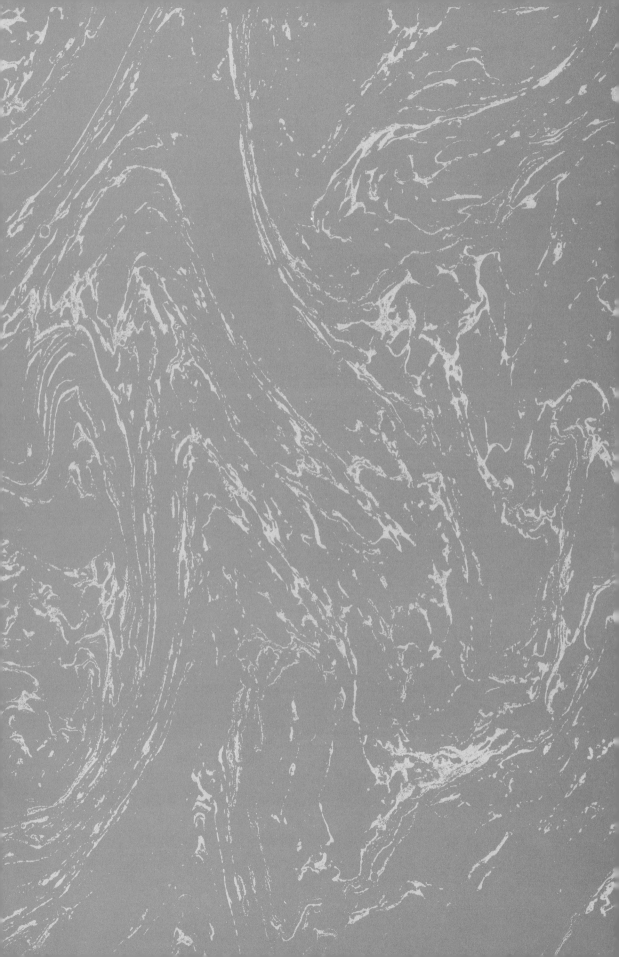